DEADLY DISEASES AND EPIDEMICS

HEPATITIS

SECOND EDITION

DEADLY DISEASES AND EPIDEMICS

Anthrax, Second Edition

Antibiotic-Resistant Bacteria

Avian Flu

Botulism, Second Edition

Campylobacteriosis

Cervical Cancer

Chicken Pox

Cholera, Second Edition

Dengue Fever and Other Hemorrhagic Viruses

Diphtheria

Ebola

Encephalitis

Escherichia coli Infections, Second Edition

Gonorrhea

Hantavirus Pulmonary Syndrome

Helicobacter pylori

Hepatitis, Second Edition

Herpes

HIV/AIDS

Infectious Diseases of the Mouth

Infectious Fungi

Influenza, Second Edition

Legionnaires' Disease

Leprosy

Lung Cancer

Lyme Disease

Mad Cow Disease

Malaria, Second Edition

Meningitis, Second Edition

Mononucleosis, Second Edition

Pelvic Inflammatory Disease

Plague, Second Edition

Polio, Second Edition

Prostate Cancer

Rabies

Rocky Mountain Spotted Fever

Rubella and Rubeola

Salmonella

SARS, Second Edition

Smallpox

Staphylococcus aureus Infections

Streptococcus (Group A), Second Edition

Streptococcus (Group B)

Syphilis, Second Edition

Tetanus

Toxic Shock Syndrome

Trypanosomiasis

Tuberculosis

Tularemia

Typhoid Fever

West Nile Virus

Whooping Cough

Yellow Fever

DEADLY DISEASES AND EPIDEMICS

HEPATITIS

SECOND EDITION

Lyle W. Horn, Ph.D., and
Alan Hecht, D.C.

Consulting Editor
Hilary Babcock, M.D., M.P.H.,
Infectious Diseases Division,
Washington University School of Medicine,
Medical Director of Occupational Health (Infectious Diseases),
Barnes–Jewish Hospital and St. Louis Children's Hospital

Foreword by
David Heymann
World Health Organization

Hepatitis, Second Edition

Chelsea House
An imprint of Infobase Learning
132 West 31st Street
New York NY 10001

Library of Congress Cataloging-in-Publication Data

Horn, Lyle W.
Hepatitis / Lyle W. Horn and Alan Hecht ; consulting editor, Hilary Babcock ; foreword by David Heymann.—2nd ed.
p. cm.—(Deadly diseases and epidemics)
Includes bibliographical references and index.
ISBN-13: 978-1-61753-016-6 (hardcover : alk. paper)
ISBN-10: 1-61753-016-6 (hardcover : alk. paper) 1. Hepatitis. I. Hecht, Alan. II. Title.
RC848.H42H67 2011
616.3'623—dc22 2011011158

Chelsea House books are available at special discounts when purchased in bulk quantities for businesses, associations, institutions, or sales promotions. Please call our Special Sales Department in New York at (212) 967-8800 or (800) 322-8755.

You can find Chelsea House on the World Wide Web at http://www.infobaselearning.com

Text design by Terry Mallon
Cover design by Takeshi Takahashi
Composition by Newgen North America
Cover printed by Yurchak Printing, Landisville, Pa.
Book printed and bound by Yurchak Printing, Landisville, Pa.
Date printed: August 2011
Printed in the United States of America

10 9 8 7 6 5 4 3 2 1

This book is printed on acid-free paper.

All links and Web addresses were checked and verified to be correct at the time of publication. Because of the dynamic nature of the Web, some addresses and links may have changed since publication and may no longer be valid.

Table of Contents

Foreword

Communicable diseases kill and cause long-term disability. The microbial agents that cause them are dynamic, changeable, and resilient: They are responsible for more than 14 million deaths each year mainly in developing countries.

Approximately 46 percent of all deaths in the developing world are due to communicable diseases, and almost 90 percent of these deaths are from AIDS, tuberculosis, malaria, and acute diarrheal and respiratory infections of children. In addition to causing great human suffering these high-mortality communicable diseases have become major obstacles to economic development. They are a challenge to control either because of the lack of effective vaccines, or because the drugs that are used to treat them are becoming less effective because of antimicrobial drug resistance.

Millions of people, especially those who are poor and living in developing countries, are also at risk from disabling communicable diseases such as polio, leprosy, lymphatic filariasis, and onchocerciasis. In addition to human suffering and permanent disability, these communicable diseases create an economic burden—both on the workforce that handicapped persons are unable to join, and on their families and society, upon which they must often depend for economic support.

Finally, the entire world is at risk of the unexpected communicable diseases, those that are called emerging or reemerging infections. Infection is often unpredictable because risk factors for transmission are not understood, or because it often results from organisms that cross the species barrier from animals to humans. The cause is often viral, such as Ebola and Marburg hemorrhagic fevers and severe acute respiratory syndrome (SARS). In addition to causing human suffering and death, these infections place health workers at great risk and are costly to economies. Infections such as bovine spongiform encephalopathy (BSE) and the associated new human variant of Creutzfeldt-Jakob disease (vCJD) in Europe. and avian influenza A (H5N1) in Asia, are reminders of the seriousness of emerging and re-emerging infections. In addition, many of these infections have the potential to cause pandemics, which are a constant threat to our economies and public health security.

Science has given us vaccines and anti-infective drugs that have helped keep infectious diseases under control. Nothing demonstrates the effectiveness of vaccines better than the successful eradication of smallpox, the decrease in polio as the eradication program continues, and the decrease in measles when routine immunization programs are supplemented by mass vaccination campaigns.

Likewise, the effectiveness of anti-infective drugs is clearly demonstrated through prolonged life or better health in those infected with viral diseases such as AIDS, parasitic infections such as malaria, and bacterial infections such as tuberculosis and pneumococcal pneumonia.

But current research and development is not filling the pipeline for new anti-infective drugs as rapidly as resistance is developing, nor is vaccine development providing vaccines for some of the most common and lethal communicable diseases. At the same time, providing people with access to existing anti-infective drugs, vaccines, and goods such as condoms or bed nets—necessary for the control of communicable diseases in many developing countries—remains a great challenge.

Education, experimentation, and the discoveries that grow from them are the tools needed to combat high mortality infectious diseases, diseases that cause disability, or emerging and re-emerging infectious diseases. At the same time, partnerships between developing and industrialized countries can overcome many of the challenges of access to goods and technologies. This book may inspire its readers to set out on the path of drug and vaccine development, or on the path to discovering better public health technologies by applying our current understanding of the human genome and those of various infectious agents. Readers may likewise be inspired to help ensure wider access to those protective goods and technologies. Such inspiration, with pragmatic action, will keep us on the winning side of the struggle against communicable diseases.

David L. Heymann
Assistant Director General
Health Security and Environment
Representative of the Director General for Polio Eradication
World Health Organization
Geneva, Switzerland

1

Introduction to Hepatitis

Mike was a junior at a large high school and a starting forward on the soccer team. Near the end of his junior year, he met some cousins of a friend at a party. He spent a lot of time talking with them because they were really into music and had friends who were members of popular bands. As the party was winding down, they invited Mike to stay a while and do some cocaine with them. Mike declined, but they assured him that it was not dangerous if you were careful and that they had been doing it for a long time and were not addicts. They really raved about the experience. Mike was curious and so he agreed to try it. Mike, his friend, and the two cousins gathered around the kitchen table. Cocaine was poured out into four lines on the table. Each young man inhaled (snorted) his line through a special straw and passed the straw to the next person. Mike was the last to snort. Mike felt the surge his friends told him to expect, but he found it disturbing rather than pleasurable. He hated the sense of losing control of himself. He felt guilty about trying the drug and had no desire to do it again. It was just a stupid experiment that he tried in a weak moment, he reasoned. So Mike went on with his life.

Mike had a great summer. He went to soccer camp, where he learned new ball-handling techniques and defensive maneuvers. Then he went on a long camping trip in Montana, where he did a lot of hiking and fishing. When he returned home, he was eager to start his senior year and play soccer. The team workouts went well for Mike until the first week of September. He suddenly found it increasingly difficult to keep up his usual pace during scrimmages and went home after practice feeling really tired. He also began to have a hard time getting up for school in the morning and felt exhausted all day. His coach noticed the change in Mike. Mike's soccer play had become so poor that the coach didn't start him in the first game. The coach knew this tiredness was not normal for Mike, so he urged Mike to see a doctor and he called Mike's parents.

Mike's doctor talked with him for a long time to get some clues about the cause of the unusual fatigue. When a patient complains of fatigue and has no other symptoms, a diagnosis can be very difficult to make. Sixty or more medical conditions have fatigue as a major symptom. Most of these diseases could be ruled out for Mike based on his general condition and medical history. Mike's doctor knew that he had been immunized for hepatitis A and hepatitis B as a young child. So Mike was checked for some other diseases that cause serious fatigue. He was tested for Lyme disease because he had spent so much time outdoors and might have been bitten by an infected deer tick, but the test result was negative. His thyroid gland was also checked and found to be normal. Mike's muscle strength was excellent, his heart was healthy, his blood pressure was fine, he did not have diabetes or infectious mononucleosis, and he was not anemic (having low levels of iron in the blood). Fatigue is associated with all of these diseases, but none affected Mike; he just felt tired.

When his doctor asked whether he had ever used drugs, Mike was embarrassed and did not answer honestly. After all, he had only experimented with cocaine once. The doctor asked if he had had a blood transfusion or been stuck with a syringe needle within the past year. Had he been tattooed or had his ears pierced? All the answers were no. Mike thought these were weird questions, but the doctor was trying to determine whether Mike might have been exposed to viruses that are present in the blood and can infect the body only by direct entry into the blood.

About 500 million people throughout the world are infected by one of six hepatitis viruses. This disease causes much suffering and has many unique features. But what is hepatitis?

Hepatitis is an **inflammation** of the liver (in Latin, *hepaticus* means "of the liver") caused either by a toxic (poisonous or harmful) substance or by a viral infection. Besides causing direct damage to the liver, toxic substances can also aggravate a viral infection. An example of a toxic substance is alcohol. Taken in moderation, alcohol is regarded as safe, but when abused or taken along with some medications, or when taken by people who have certain diseases, it can cause complications. For instance, even just a little alcohol consumed by a person who has viral hepatitis can rapidly cause severe liver damage. This book discusses only viral hepatitides (plural of *hepatitis*) because these diseases are of major importance for public health worldwide and because their causes have one thing in common—viral infection.

Five different viruses—designated A, B, C, D, and E—are known to cause hepatitis; a sixth virus, G, is associated with hepatitis but has not been shown to cause serious **clinical disease**. There have even been some reports of a seventh virus, F. These reports are not confirmed, and health experts do not accept it as a unique virus.

All forms of viral hepatitis have common symptoms, but each also has its own special features. Recognizing these features helps us understand how the disease is transmitted, how it affects us, how it can be treated, and how we can prevent it.

Viruses that infect through the blood are referred to as **bloodborne**, and their transmission, which occurs by any route other than through the intestines, is referred to as **parenteral transmission**. Common parenteral routes include puncture by an object contaminated by a virus such as a needle, or direct exposure of an open wound or sore to an object contaminated with blood.

Poor countries are likely to have water contaminated by human feces. Many viruses are passed out of the body (shed) in the stool and can be transmitted through a simple act such as eating fresh vegetables that were washed with contaminated water. Consumption of contaminated water or food allows these viruses to enter the body from the gut. This route of transmission is referred to as **enteric** (relating to the intestine).

The first tests for viral hepatitis are serological (pertaining to blood serum). **Serum** (plasma) is the liquid part of whole blood that remains after all blood cells and clotting materials are removed. When a person is infected by a **microbe** (a microorganism that does not have a nucleus), **proteins** (large functional and structural molecules in cells and body fluids) called **antigens**, which are made by the microbe, are found in the serum. These signal the presence of a substance foreign to the immune system. Other proteins called **antibodies** are produced by the immune system in response to antigens and may also be present in the blood. Antigens and the antibodies made to fight the foreign microbe are specific. That is, a particular microbe antigen is not found on any other microbe, and the antibodies produced in response to the antigen recognize only that antigen. It is these antibodies that are detected by serological tests. These tests may be followed by other tests for proteins that are released from injured liver cells and for **viral nucleic acid** that is specific to a virus. Finally, a **liver biopsy** (sampling of liver tissue) may be done to determine the extent of liver damage.

It turned out that Mike's serological test results were positive for the acute hepatitis. Fatigue became so bad that he had to quit the soccer team and his schoolwork deteriorated.

There is no treatment that can cure acute hepatitis. All doctors can do is treat the symptoms. Mike was advised to get lots of rest, to eat properly, to refrain from alcohol under any circumstances because it can aggravate the disease and cause liver failure very rapidly, and avoid strenuous exercise until he felt better. He was also instructed about how to prevent spreading his disease to his family and others. Mike was referred to a liver disease specialist who would assess Mike's status regularly.

Mike slowly recovered his stamina over a period of six months, although his energy level was not what it once was. He was able to improve his schoolwork and participate in normal social activities, but he had to forget about sports during his senior year.

2

The Phases of Hepatitis and Their Common Symptoms

Jackie began to feel like she was coming down with the flu. Her body ached, she had a low-grade fever, a headache, and felt tired and weak. She went to bed and figured that with some rest and plenty of fluids, she'd get over it within a few days.

After a week, Jackie was over the original symptoms, but she noticed that her appetite was waning and she was losing weight. In addition, her skin began to itch and she realized that it was beginning to look somewhat yellow. She also began to notice that her abdomen was feeling tender. This caused her a great deal of alarm and she immediately went to see her physician.

As soon as the doctor looked at Jackie he suspected one of the forms of hepatitis based on her appearance and description of her symptoms. He drew a sample of her blood and sent it right out to the lab. A few days later the results showed that she was suffering from hepatitis A. The question was, how did she contract it? As it turned out, Jackie had eaten at a local restaurant where several other patrons had also developed hepatitis A. Health department investigators tracked the virus to one of the food preparers who was infected with the virus.

Acute viral hepatitis is the initial short-term stage of the disease. It begins with the entry of the virus into the body and continues for up to six months. Jackie's experience was typical of a person in an **acute** phase of hepatitis. All forms of viral hepatitis (A to E) have an acute phase. Symptoms may or may not appear during this phase.

Chronic hepatitis refers to a continuing lifelong infection. The diagnosis of chronic hepatitis is made only when the **clinical signs** (abnormalities that can be discovered by examination) and **symptoms** (abnormalities that are sensed by the patient) have lasted more than six months. Hepatitis viruses B, C, and D are known to cause chronic hepatitis; the others do not. Chronic hepatitis does not always develop because a person's immune system may successfully defeat the virus. But it can develop when a person's immune system is unable to eliminate the invading virus. When the virus avoids detection by not producing proteins (antigens) that allow the immune system to recognize it as an invader or by constantly changing (mutating) the antigens it produces or by reproducing faster than the immune system is able to attack and destroy the virus, chronic hepatitis can occur. Symptoms may first appear, continue, or disappear during the chronic phase. Sometimes they come and go. The absence of symptoms does not mean there is no disease. It is not understood why the symptoms of hepatitis are erratic.

Some people infected with hepatitis don't experience any symptoms until late in the chronic phase (20 or more years after infection). This symptom-free experience is most common during the acute phase in infants and young children, but it can also be possible for adults. The reasons why a person is symptom-free are not understood, but the fact that symptom-free disease occurs is important for understanding the impact of hepatitis on the patient and on public health.

Infected people who are symptom-free may discover only by chance that they have been infected. Doctors do not check for hepatitis during routine physical examinations. However, all donated blood is checked for hepatitis B and C, so a blood donor may receive a letter from the Red Cross or a local hospital informing him or her of the presence of hepatitis infection. Life insurance companies often require tests for hepatitis before issuing a policy to an applicant. A person may go to the doctor complaining of flu-like symptoms, and the doctor may decide to check for hepatitis when no influenza infection is found. The patient may then learn that he or she has viral hepatitis.

The severity of symptoms varies a great deal among individuals with viral hepatitis. Some people never have symptoms. When symptoms do occur, not all known symptoms are necessarily experienced. Some people experience only mild flu-like discomfort and go about their daily lives without interruption. Others see a physician and have to rest in bed for a few days to several weeks. In rare cases, a person has to be hospitalized. Although there are exceptions, the older a person is when infected, the more likely he or she is to have serious symptoms. The reasons why this is true are not understood.

Nevertheless, studies have been performed that support this fact. For example, one study showed that in 180 cases of acute hepatitis A, hospitalization rates increased with age. The rate for those in the 40–49 year old group was only 3% while the rate in the 50–69 year old group was 12%. The highest rate of hospitalization was seen in patients ≥ 70 years old with a 42% hospitalization rate associated with an infection with hepatitis A.[1] Possibly, as we age, our immune system becomes less effective.

Except for hepatitis C, for which there are new treatments, no treatment can rid our bodies entirely of hepatitis virus infection. Only our own immune system can defeat hepatitis A and B. When the immune system defeats a viral infection, it is said that the disease is **self-limited**. Treatment relieves discomfort and symptoms and addresses changes in body functions that could cause death. Reduction of fever, replacement of body fluids and intravenous feeding, and support of breathing with a respirator may be required. A liver transplant is a last resort in some cases.

A PUBLIC HEALTH PROBLEM

Communicable diseases that are symptom-free are a serious public health problem. A person who is unaware of being infected may spread the disease widely. Virus-infected, symptom-free people who have had the disease for at least six months are called "carriers" of the virus. One of the most common ways that hepatitis was transmitted in the past was by blood transfusion. Unaware of his or her hepatitis infection, a carrier would donate blood, which would then be given to someone in need. Viral hepatitis would then develop very quickly, sometimes within a week of the transfusion, and place patients who were already seriously ill at great risk. It has become routine in developed countries to screen donated blood for hepatitis B since about 1972, when an economical and reliable test became available, and for hepatitis C since 1992. Screening is routine only in developed countries, however, because the cost is too high and laboratory facilities are not available in many poor countries. The incidence of hepatitis after blood transfusion in developed countries fell markedly after blood screening began. According to the Centers for Disease Control and Prevention (CDC), before blood screening began in the 1980s, there was an average of 242,000 new hepatitis C infections per year in the United States, but the number dropped to 36,000 per year by 1996, four years after routine blood screening began.

ACUTE PHASES OF INFECTION

Acute viral hepatitis can be divided into four phases. The **incubation phase** begins with the initial infection and continues until the onset of symptoms or, if no symptoms appear, until blood tests show that the person's immune system has begun to fight the virus. This phase can last from one week to many months, depending on the kind of virus and the number of viral microbes the person was infected with. The larger the dose of these microbes, the shorter the incubation period. Hepatitis after blood transfusion, for example, develops within a week because the viral dose received by transfusion is very large. During this phase, the virus reproduces rapidly and the infected person may be highly contagious. This period is dangerous for others because the infected person does not know about the infection and cannot take precautions to avoid passing it on.

The **prodromal phase** starts with the onset of symptoms, although we know that not all people experience symptoms. In Jackie's case, the symptom was feeling like she had the flu. A person may think he or she has a mild case of the flu, which may include a low-grade fever. This may be followed within days by anorexia (loss of appetite), malaise (feeling "down" with fatigue and no energy), and nausea and vomiting. Smokers often lose their desire to smoke.

During the prodromal phase, the blood levels of some proteins that are made by the liver rise. This is because the body's immune response to the virus actually causes damage to liver cells. One of the most important of these proteins is an enzyme called **alanine aminotransferase** or ALT. ALT is involved in the normal chemical processing of the amino acid alanine. It converts alanine to carbon dioxide and water and provides useful energy for the cell. Doctors may monitor the blood levels of ALT in a patient they know has hepatitis to follow the progress of the infection. However, a single measurement of blood ALT cannot provide diagnostic evidence of hepatitis.

Another enzyme that is measured is aspartate aminotransferase or AST. This enzyme acts to convert the amino acid aspartate and the Krebs cycle intermediate alpha-ketoglutarate into the citric acid cycle intermediate oxaloacetate and the amino acid glutamate and vice versa. Although less specific than ALT because it is also found in the heart, skeletal muscles, brain, blood cells, and kidneys, the two enzymes are often measured when liver damage is suspected. Frequently, an AST/ALT ratio is calculated in order to distinguish between different causes of liver damage.

Three to 10 days after the first symptoms of hepatitis appear, the **icteric phase** of infection may begin. The word *icteric* means "jaundiced" and refers to changes in the color of urine, stools, skin, and sclerae (whites of the eyes). The urine may turn very dark yellow at first. The stools may become pale or light yellow or may be described as clay-like. Yellow skin may not be obvious, but often yellowing can be seen underneath the fingernails

ENZYMES

Enzymes are proteins that carry out very specific chemical reactions in the cell with high efficiency and speed. A chemical reaction is a process by which two or more different chemicals interact to form new chemicals. Many chemical reactions in the body could not occur, or would proceed too slowly for practical use, without the aid of enzymes. They are essential for normal cell function. Thousands of enzymes are known, and each one is dedicated to a single chemical reaction. One seemingly simple process, such as the conversion of a sugar molecule to carbon dioxide and water, can actually involve about two dozen separate chemical reactions, each requiring a specific enzyme. Enzymes are required to make nucleic acids (DNA and RNA) and proteins; to make amino acids, which are the building blocks of all proteins; to manufacture or destroy a long list of chemical substances; to make our muscles shorten and develop force; and to facilitate many other essential processes that are too numerous to list. Not all enzymes are found in every cell of our body. Cells make only the enzymes they need to perform their specific functions. Alanine aminotransferase (ALT) is an important enzyme for normal liver function, for example, but is not very important in a skin or muscle cell. When a cell is sick or dying, enzymes leak out of the cell and into the blood. Knowledge of the blood level of an enzyme such as ALT can give clues to the degree of cell damage that has occurred in an organ that is known to use that enzyme.

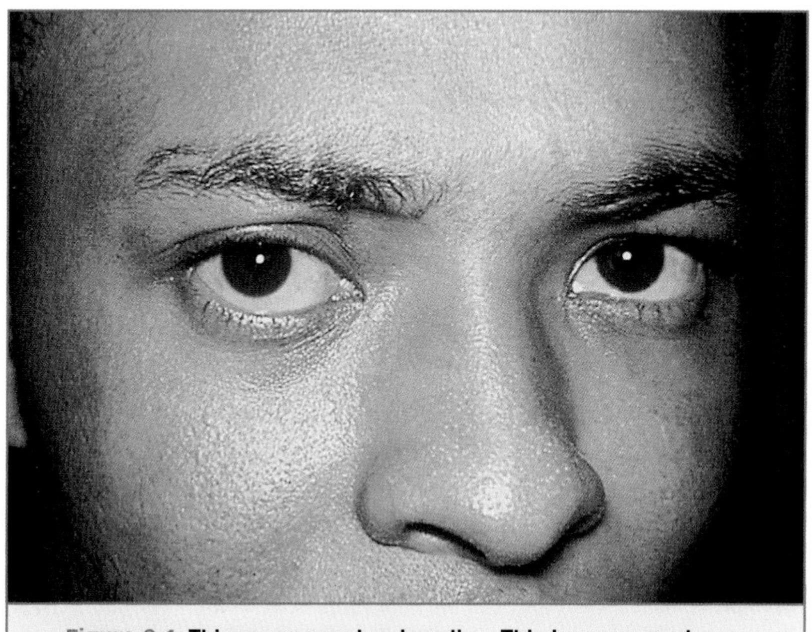

Figure 2.1 **This young man has jaundice. This is a very good example of the "yellowing" caused by jaundice. The sclerae (whites of the eyes) are obviously yellow. Healthy "whites" of the eyes are truly white. This feature stands out most prominently in this person. A closer look will show that his skin, especially his nose and around the eyes, has a yellow tone. An even closer look will show that the moist tissues on the edges of his lower eyelids are also yellowed. These tissues are normally pink. (Centers for Disease Control and Prevention)**

or in the sclerae (Figure 2.1). Most people with hepatitis do not develop **jaundice**, but it is still common enough that it is considered an important sign. During the icteric phase, the symptoms that appeared during the earlier prodromal phase may fade and be replaced by itching on the body trunk. The jaundice itself is at its worst about one to two weeks after the start of the icteric phase, and then usually fades over a period of four to eight weeks.

Eventually, if the infection is self-limited, the immune system begins to win the battle against the virus and ultimately

BILIRUBIN

The cause of yellowing, or jaundice, is an excess of the chemical bilirubin in blood and urine. Bilirubin is a product of the breakdown of red blood cells. Red blood cells contain hemoglobin, which is a protein whose primary function is to bind oxygen for transport from the lungs to the rest of the body. The key part of hemoglobin for binding oxygen is called the heme group. The heme group contains one iron ion. Bilirubin is a remnant of the heme group without the iron ion that results from the destruction of hemoglobin. It is normally taken up from the blood by the liver, modified chemically, and excreted by way of the bile into the small intestine and thus in the feces. Modified bilirubin is further changed to other chemicals in the gut such as stercobilinogen, which gives the normal stool its typical brown color. In a normal adult, about 0.2 grams (g) of bilirubin is excreted in the stool every day.

When liver cells are not functioning properly, release of modified bilirubin may be impaired. Considerable amounts of bilirubin are not taken up at all by the liver, and modified bilirubin is released back to the blood. As a consequence, the modified and unmodified bilirubin build up in the blood. Both of these chemicals have a yellow color. The excess bilirubin can move out of the blood into the tissues, where it causes yellow discoloration, and is excreted by the kidneys into the urine, which accounts for the dark yellow color of urine during jaundice. Reduced excretion of bilirubin into the gut during liver disease results in less stercobilinogen, or brown pigment, and a lighter-colored stool.

triumphs. This is the final phase of acute hepatitis, the **recovery phase**, which typically lasts four to eight weeks but can last up to six months. Symptoms slowly fade away, including jaundice. During this phase, the liver may be enlarged (**hepatomegaly**) and tender to the touch, so that a person may feel discomfort just below the right ribs with slight pressure. Fatigue may be the last symptom to disappear. Finally, all symptoms disappear, and the person returns to normal health with immunity to future infections by the same kind of virus. **Immunity** means that the immune system remembers the specific antigens of a microbe and can be reactivated quickly to fight a new invasion by that organism. Antibodies may also remain in the blood indefinitely, so that they can immediately attack any reinvading organisms.

COMPLICATIONS OF THE ACUTE PHASE

A rare and fatal complication that can develop during the acute phase of hepatitis is known as **fulminant hepatitis.** *Fulminant* means sudden and explosive, like a lightning strike. This complication is most often associated with hepatitis B (1% of cases), but can also develop with hepatitides A and C. Death can occur within two weeks of onset. It is not understood how fulminant hepatitis develops, and there is no cure. Liver cells are destroyed very rapidly and liver size decreases dramatically (known as acute yellow atrophy). The liver ceases to provide essential functions for the rest of the body, and toxic substances build up in the blood. These toxic materials enter the brain and cause **hepatic encephalopathy,** a disorder of the brain caused by a malfunctioning liver. An irreversible coma can develop within hours. The pressure of fluids in the brain builds up and causes physical damage to brain cells directly and reduces blood flow to the brain. This results in additional brain cell damage and death due to lack of oxygen. The toxic substances can also promote kidney failure, which can be fatal. However, in some cases that are caught early enough, a liver transplant may save the patient's life. Survival generally is not common; it is most likely in children and extremely rare in adults. A lucky few recover completely, have no permanent damage to the liver or brain, and have no chronic viral infection.

CHRONIC PHASES OF INFECTION

Chronic hepatitis begins after six months of infection without recovery. Chronic hepatitis can be divided into three phases. The first is the **replicative phase**, during which the virus reproduces itself actively and infects healthy liver cells. This phase can last several years, resulting in a large amount of virus in the blood (**viremia**). The disease is most contagious during this phase. The **seroconversion phase** follows the replicative phase. During this phase, the immune system attacks and destroys about 10% of infected liver cells each year. Usually, an infected person has no symptoms during the seroconversion phase and the person also has less viremia, although blood levels of ALT are high because of the destruction of liver cells. Finally, the **nonreplicative phase** sets in, during which the virus stops reproducing and viremia is minimal. However, replication may be spontaneously reactivated at any time for reasons that are not understood.

Replication reactivation, although usually spontaneous (occurring in approximately 50% of cases), may be brought about by several different known factors mostly related to suppression of the immune system. Reactivation may be seen in cases of both hepatitis B and hepatitis C. Cancer chemotherapy in patients with a history of hepatitis B is one probable cause. Chemotherapy inhibits cytotoxic T cell activity in the liver, thus allowing the virus to reactivate. This is particularly true in cases of hepatitis B where the patient's condition usually worsens during the reactivation process.[2]

Another likely cause of reactivation is corticosteroid therapy for some other condition. This type of therapy should be avoided unless it's being used as a lifesaving therapy, particularly in cases of hepatitis B. Corticosteroids suppress the immune system and will allow the virus to reactivate.[3]

Hepatitis C virus reactivation has been shown to occur spontaneously at a high rate when a specific genotype of the virus is infecting patients. In a study done on patients with genotype 2c hepatitis C there was a significant percentage of reactivation compared to genotype 1b hepatitis C virus patients. In looking at other possible factors, there was no correlation between reactivation and sex, age, modality, or duration of infection.[4]

The symptoms of chronic viral hepatitis include those suffered in the acute phase. They may come and go and often are not as severe as in the acute phase, but there will always be some degree of viremia. A person may be symptom-free for many years. Others may suffer from persistent symptoms, especially fatigue. Jaundice may reappear and, if it does, it is considered a serious sign of advanced disease. Hepatomegaly (an enlarged liver) may persist or get worse. Some people may live a normal life span without serious consequences. In others, the disease progresses very slowly to a stage in which liver failure may cause death. The likelihood of this happening depends on which hepatitis virus the person is infected with and whether the infection is properly treated. In the United States, infection with hepatitis C virus is most likely to lead to death because the treatments for hepatitis C are less effective than treatment for hepatitis B. About 70% of deaths caused by chronic hepatitis in the United States are caused by hepatitis C. The National Institute of Diabetes and Digestive and Kidney Diseases has estimated that there are between 10,000 and 12,000 deaths annually in the United States caused by chronic hepatitis C virus infections.[5]

COMPLICATIONS OF THE CHRONIC PHASE

The first serious complication that may develop in the chronic phase of hepatitis, 10 or more years after infection, is **cirrhosis**. Cirrhosis is end-stage liver disease and has many possible causes—chronic viral hepatitis being one and alcohol abuse being the most common. *End-stage* means the end of life. At least 20% of chronic hepatitis cases lead to cirrhosis. *Cirrhosis* means "yellow condition" and refers to the dull orange-yellow appearance of the diseased liver, which is caused in this case by deposits of large amounts of fat. There is massive damage to liver cells, caused mainly by the immune system's unrelenting attempt to eliminate the virus. Immune cells called killer T cells attack and destroy the infected liver cells rather than destroying the virus directly. In this way, the body attacks itself. As a result, the body attempts to repair the damaged liver cells by forming scar tissue in the liver. This reaction is similar to scab formation after an injury to the skin. In turn, the blood supply to many parts of the organ is disrupted by the scarring, leading to loss of function and further cell death. Cirrhosis ranks third as a cause of death in the Western world, after heart disease and cancer, in people aged 45 to 65 years and 12th as a cause of death among people of all ages. It ranks 8th as a cause of death in the United States. There is no cure for cirrhosis. A liver transplant may be lifesaving if the person's overall condition has not deteriorated too much and a suitable donor can be found.

A second serious complication in chronic hepatitis, which usually develops more slowly and appears later than cirrhosis, is a liver cancer known as **hepatocellular carcinoma**. The name simply means that the cancer arises from the liver cells themselves (the **hepatocytes**). Having cirrhosis is thought to greatly increase the risk of cancer, but it is not necessary for cancer to occur. Hepatocellular carcinoma is incurable and fatal and is most likely to occur in people with the chronic hepatitides B and C who are between 35 and 65 years old. About 30% of cases of chronic hepatitis B and 10% of cases of chronic hepatitis C proceed to liver cancer. In these cases, a liver transplant may be lifesaving.

There is a vaccine available for prevention of hepatitis B. This vaccine was the first one of just a few vaccines that actually can prevent a cancer, which it does by preventing hepatitis B.

In summary, viral hepatitis has both an acute phase, which develops in everyone who gets infected, and a chronic phase, which does not always develop and occurs only with the hepatitis B, C, and D viruses. The acute phase typically lasts six months or less, whereas the chronic phase may last a lifetime. The most common symptoms are malaise or fatigue, low-grade fever, jaundice, and nausea and vomiting. Most cases of hepatitis are resolved by the end of the acute phase because the immune system successfully eliminates the virus. These infections are self-limited. A person is then immune to another infection by the same virus. An infected person in the chronic phase may never experience symptoms or may do so only very late in life. In others, symptoms may come and go, or they may be persistent, especially fatigue. Chronic hepatitis may progress after 10 or more years to cirrhosis and after 20 or more years to liver cancer. Both complications are usually fatal, although a liver transplant may save the life of the person infected.

3

Looking at the Liver

Matt had developed severe kidney disease following a series of strep throats when he was a young boy. Eventually, both kidneys failed and he needed a transplant. Unfortunately, the transplant didn't come through, leaving him to rely on renal dialysis three times each week for many years.

Somewhere during the years that he was repeatedly connected to the dialysis machine with a needle in a shunt in his arm, he contracted hepatitis C from equipment that was not properly cleaned. As time went on, the condition of his liver deteriorated. At first he became fatigued, then he developed mild pain over the area where his liver was. Eventually, he lost his appetite and suffered from muscle and joint pains.

As the years went on his condition worsened until he developed cirrhosis of the liver. He became more and more despondent and depressed. His outlook on life was bleak and he wondered just how much time he had left to live.

His prognosis continued to decline until one day his doctor called him at home to give him wonderful news. A donor was found whose tissue type very closely matched Matt's and he was to report to the hospital for a liver transplant. All at once, his attitude changed drastically and he realized that he now would have a future.

UNIQUENESS OF THE LIVER

The liver is the largest organ by weight in the body. The average weight of the liver in a healthy adult is about 3 pounds (1.36 kg). This remarkable organ performs many functions that are essential for life. One of its amazing properties is its ability to **regenerate** (rebuild and restore to its original structure and function). It is the only human organ that can do this when a large amount of tissue is involved. If some of the liver is removed surgically, the remaining liver can regrow and function normally. It is also true that the liver can lose 75% of its cells before it stops functioning. This fact is extremely important for understanding the long-term, or chronic, effects of viral hepatitis.

The liver is found in the upper third of the abdomen. It rests on the stomach, the intestines, and the right kidney. It is divided into two large subunits called **lobes**. The right lobe is the larger of the two and is separated from the left lobe by a large ligament (falciform ligament) that also attaches the liver to the diaphragm and abdominal wall. Both of these lobes are close to the diaphragm. There are two other lobes that are small and are located underneath the major lobes: the caudate lobe and the quadrate lobe (Figure 3.1). Four other ligaments also attach the lobes to the abdominal wall. The normal liver is dark red-brown in color.

The liver is supplied by the **hepatic artery**, which provides the oxygenated blood the liver needs, and the hepatic and **portal veins**. The portal vein delivers all of the blood that flows through the intestines to the liver. This blood carries all the nutrients that have been recovered from the intestines. Everything we eat or ingest that can enter the blood must first flow through the liver. Portal blood accounts for 80% of the blood supplied to the liver, with the artery supplying the rest. The **hepatic vein** collects all the blood supplied to the liver and returns it to the heart. At any instant, about 13% of the body's blood is in the liver. The hepatic **bile duct** is another important tube that leaves the liver. This tube collects all the **bile** produced by the liver and delivers it to the common bile duct that carries it to the small intestine just beyond the stomach. Attached to the bile duct is the gallbladder, which serves as a storage reservoir for bile when it is not needed in the gut for digestion of fats. About half of the bile produced by the liver first goes into the gallbladder. When we eat fatty food, the fat triggers a

(continues on page 29)

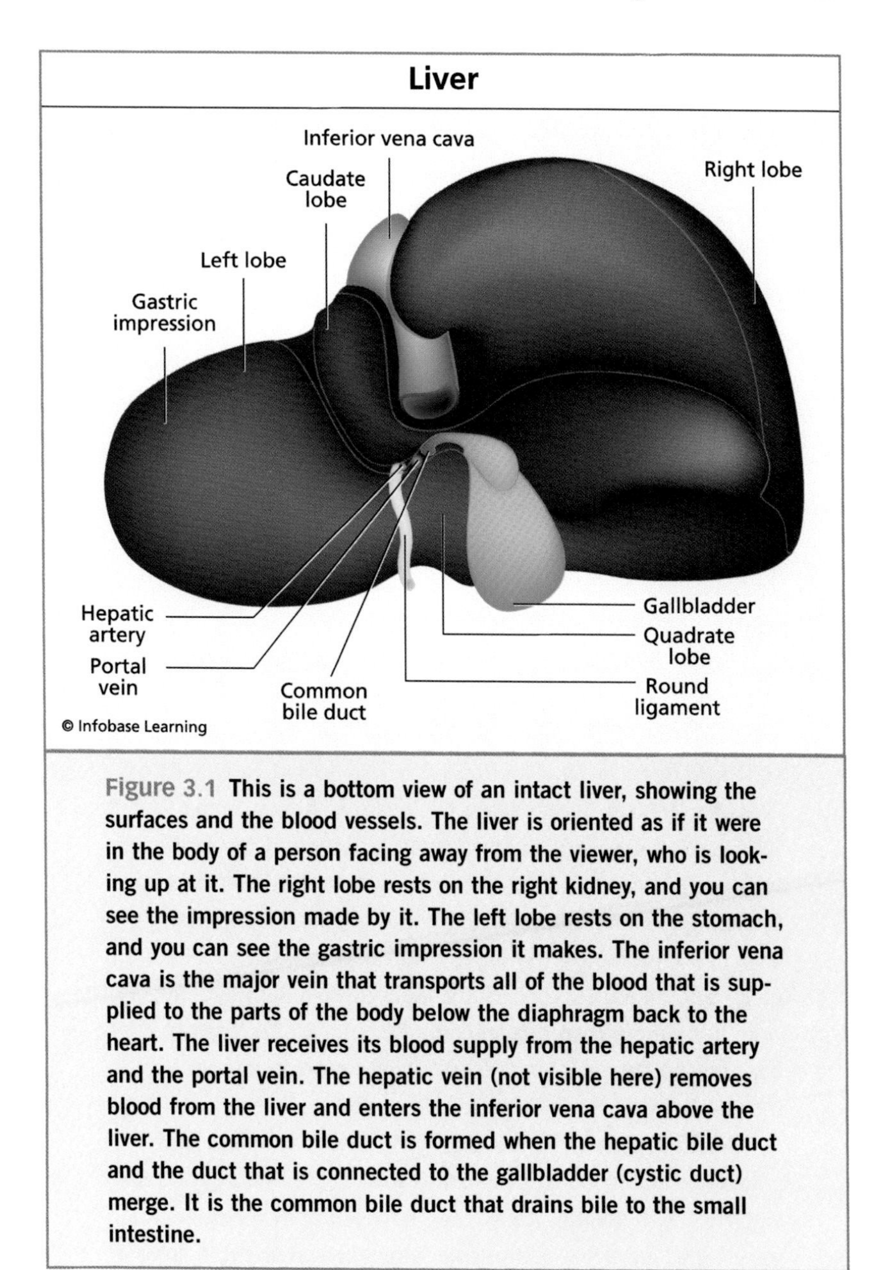

Figure 3.1 This is a bottom view of an intact liver, showing the surfaces and the blood vessels. The liver is oriented as if it were in the body of a person facing away from the viewer, who is looking up at it. The right lobe rests on the right kidney, and you can see the impression made by it. The left lobe rests on the stomach, and you can see the gastric impression it makes. The inferior vena cava is the major vein that transports all of the blood that is supplied to the parts of the body below the diaphragm back to the heart. The liver receives its blood supply from the hepatic artery and the portal vein. The hepatic vein (not visible here) removes blood from the liver and enters the inferior vena cava above the liver. The common bile duct is formed when the hepatic bile duct and the duct that is connected to the gallbladder (cystic duct) merge. It is the common bile duct that drains bile to the small intestine.

LIVER TRANSPLANTS

Liver transplants are performed only with patients who have no other hope for survival and who meet strict technical requirements that ensure a good chance for success. The liver is the second most frequently transplanted organ (after the kidney) and the procedure has become common throughout the developed world. About 17,000 patients are eligible for a transplant every year in the United States, but only about 5,300 procedures are performed because of the limited number of donors. Usually, donors have died from causes that have not affected their livers, such as an automobile accident. Of course, these people must have completed an organ donor form or have relatives who are willing to grant permission for donation. In addition, the donor must have the same blood type and be of similar body size as the recipient.

Since 1989, it has been possible to use liver tissue from a live donor for transplants because of the healthy liver's ability to regenerate itself. The first live donor liver transplant (LDLT) was performed by Dr. Christoph Broelsch at the University of Chicago Medical Center when two-year-old Alyssa Smith, suffering with biliary atresia, was given a portion of her mother's liver and survived.[1] Up to 50% of a live donor's liver may be taken. The risk of death for the donor is about 1 chance in 100 (1%). Moreover, the donor must undergo and recover from major abdominal surgery. These facts discourage many people from donating. When the procedure is successful, both the donor's and the recipient's livers should grow to normal size within about six to eight weeks after surgery.

Another remarkable fact about the liver that makes transplants feasible is that it can survive without a blood supply for eight to 24 hours after it has been removed from the body. This means that the donor and recipient may live on opposite sides of the country without causing a problem for the procedure. Transplant surgeons prefer to use livers that have been out of the body for less than eight hours, but will use older ones if necessary.

(continued from page 26)
reflex activated by the hormone cholecystokinin that causes the gallbladder to contract and push the stored bile into the gut to help absorb the fats from the gut into the blood.

The bile duct system is like a highly branched tree. The smallest vessels, **canaliculi**, are microscopic in size and are present throughout the liver. They gradually converge into larger and larger vessels, just as the small branches of a tree converge into ever-larger branches, until finally the "trunk of the tree," or hepatic bile duct, is reached. This is a very efficient system for collecting bile from the liver cells.

The liver lobes are further subdivided into many thousands of basic functional units or small lobes called **lobules**. Lobules can only be seen clearly with a microscope. Figure 3.2 is a sketch of a typical lobule. When we look at a cross-section of a lobule, we can see a hexagonal (six-sided) boundary, a central hub or axle, and lots of "spokes" radiating between the hub and the periphery of the lobule. Open spaces between the spokes are called **sinusoids**, which means "small sinuses." A **sinus** is a cavity, channel, or hollow. The liver sinusoids are dilated blood vessels that are a location for oxygen-rich blood from the hepatic artery and nutrient-rich blood that arrives through the hepatic portal vein that arrives from the intestines. The sinusoids contain specialized cells known as Kupffer cells that are macrophages (cells that engulf and digest microorganisms and foreign particles) that destroy worn out red blood cells, bacteria, and foreign proteins.

At each of the six corners of the hexagon is a cluster of three vessels: very small branches of the hepatic artery, the portal vein, and a small bile duct. The artery and vein feed their blood into the sinusoids, where it flows slowly to the hub. The hub is called the central vein and is a very small branch of the hepatic vein. It collects the blood for return to the hepatic vein and then to the heart. The spokes form the walls of the sinusoids and are made up of hepatocytes (liver cells), which are the cells that do all the work of the liver. Their work consists of taking up materials from the blood, modifying these materials, and delivering the modified and new materials back to the blood and into the bile ducts. The bile ducts are not connected directly to the blood. They receive bile from the canaliculi between the hepatocytes, which produce and excrete

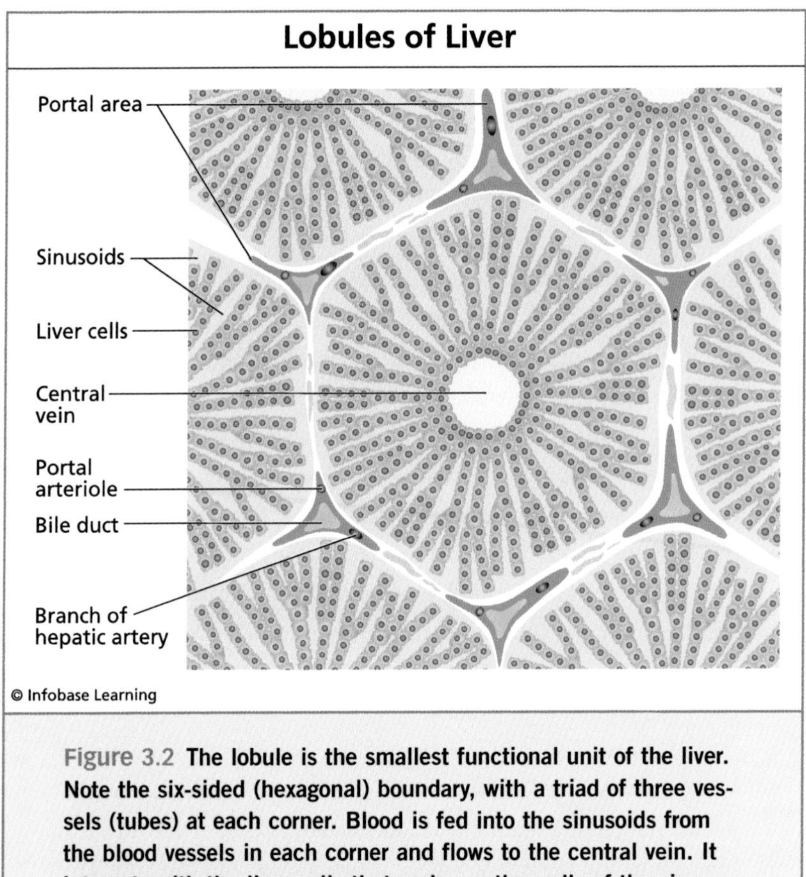

Figure 3.2 **The lobule is the smallest functional unit of the liver. Note the six-sided (hexagonal) boundary, with a triad of three vessels (tubes) at each corner. Blood is fed into the sinusoids from the blood vessels in each corner and flows to the central vein. It interacts with the liver cells that make up the walls of the sinusoids, where nutrients and waste materials are exchanged. Bile is secreted from liver cells into canaliculi (not visible) that are connected to the bile ducts in the triads.**

bile into them. It is the hepatocytes that become infected by the hepatitis viruses.

Liver specialists recognize that the liver performs more than 500 important functions. This organ is truly a chemical factory; an energy, vitamin, and mineral storage reservoir; a waste treatment plant; and a regulator of other organs. It has several major functions. The liver produces most of the important proteins that are needed in blood. It produces special proteins that carry fats throughout our body (lipoproteins). It takes up sugars from the blood and converts them into a special form (glycogen) for storage, and it breaks down the glycogen and releases sugar in the form of glucose to the blood when energy is needed by other parts of the body (glycogenolysis). It takes up from or releases to the blood amino acids as needed and regulates the blood levels of these protein building blocks. It helps to process hemoglobin (a protein-iron compound found in the blood) from dying red blood cells by saving iron for reuse and forming modified bilirubin for release to the bile. It converts ammonia, which is toxic and is released when proteins are broken down, to less toxic urea, which is returned to the blood and excreted in the urine. It produces chemicals that are essential for blood clotting (called **coagulation**) or clotting factors, and it makes bile salts for release to the bile, which are essential for the normal digestion of fats in the small intestine. The liver helps fight infections by removing and destroying bacteria from the blood and by secreting some immune factors that help the cells of the immune system fight infections. Finally, the liver removes foreign and toxic substances from the blood, including therapeutic drugs, and destroys them. Broken-down fragments of wastes and toxic substances are modified and released to the bile for ultimate disposal in the feces and to the blood where they are filtered by the kidneys for disposal in the urine.

Viral hepatitis is a serious illness because the hepatitis viruses invade the hepatocytes and interfere with their normal

BILE

Bile is a dark yellow-green, bitter, alkaline fluid secreted by liver cells into the bile ducts. It is made up of waste products, cholesterol, and bile salts. Bile drains waste from the liver into the gut for excretion in the feces. This is an extremely important mechanism for eliminating waste and toxic substances from the body. Bile salts aid in the breakdown of dietary fats in the small intestine, in the absorption of these fats into the blood, and in the transport of fat to the liver for further processing. The bile salts are recovered by the liver and recycled. Fats, especially the compounds called fatty acids, are important parts of cell structures, some hormones, chemicals used for regulation of blood pressure and the immune response, and cell metabolism. Although the body can make many fats from other chemicals, including sugars, it is more efficient to acquire them in the diet. Some fatty acids cannot be made by the human body and are called essential fatty acids because they are necessary for normal health. We must acquire these in the diet. Two examples are linoleic acid (an omega-6 fatty acid) and alpha-linolenic acid (an omega-3 fatty acid). These compounds are involved in the production of energy by cells; the exchange of oxygen between the lungs and the blood; the synthesis of hemoglobin, which is the oxygen-carrying protein in red blood cells; the regulation of cell growth and division; and nerve function.

Fats do not dissolve in water. This is a major problem when we consider how fats might be moved from the gut across the intestinal wall into the blood and be transported by the blood throughout the body, especially to the liver. The bile salts emulsify (break up or dissolve) the fats. That is, one part of the bile salt molecule binds to or dissolves in the fat and the other part dissolves in water. A very small fat droplet is surrounded by many bile salts, with part of each salt molecule dissolved in the fat and the other part dissolved in the water. One of the most important fat-binding proteins, and also the most abundant protein in blood plasma, is albumin. Albumin serves many functions in blood, including the binding and transport of fatty acids.

functions. Consequently, the liver cannot do a proper job of supporting the rest of the body. Another serious consequence of viral infection is that the immune system begins attacking and destroying the infected hepatocytes. If this goes on for less than six months, before the virus is eliminated, then the damaged liver will regenerate and there will be no long-term damage. However, some viruses cannot be eliminated completely by the immune system. Remember that up to 75% of liver cells can be lost before there is a serious loss of liver function. It may take 20 or more years for this level of liver destruction to develop, and the infected person may not know he or she is sick until liver failure starts.

4

Inflammation and the Immune Response

Julia was a teenaged drug addict who had been using several different hardcore drugs for at least six years. She often shared needles with friends, who were also addicted to drugs, without cleaning them.

One day she began to feel ill with a fever, loss of appetite, nausea, general body aches and pains, and an overall feeling of malaise. She guessed that this was all just due to severe exhaustion or possibly a bad reaction to one or more of the drugs she regularly used. She thought that maybe one of her suppliers had cut one of the drugs with some substance that was making her sick.

Her illness, however, didn't go away in a day or two as she expected, and she began to become frightened. Julia waited for a week or so in hopes that everything would clear up. When it didn't, she knew she would have to visit a doctor, but she had no medical coverage and very little money. The only option was to go to the free clinic in town and see one of its doctors.

When she arrived, looking very drawn and pale, she had the same symptoms as before with the addition of pain in the right side of her abdomen. Her skin had also begun to take on a slightly yellowish tint. She was very scared.

The doctor took time to examine her thoroughly. He drew blood to send to the lab for a number of different tests, including those that would let him know how well Julia's liver was functioning. One of the exams he performed was a physical exam that included palpating (using the fingers to feel an area) the right side of her abdomen where she had complained of pain. As he pressed on her abdomen just below the border of her rib cage, he was able to feel tissue that is not normally there. This was her liver extending below the edge of her rib cage. It was enlarged and protruding into the portion of the abdominal cavity where it was not supposed to be. He also used his fingers to tap on the whole area and heard the familiar dull thud that indicated the presence of solid tissue in an area that usually sounded hollow. There was no doubt in his mind that Julia's liver was enlarged and she most certainly had hepatitis.

Hepatitis means "inflammation of the liver." Just what is inflammation? Inflammation is a set of complex cellular and chemical reactions in blood vessels and the surrounding tissues in response to injury or to abnormal stimulation caused by chemical (such as alcohol in the liver or bee venom in the skin) or biologic agents (such as bacteria and viruses). Characteristic signs of inflammation are redness, higher-than-normal tissue warmth or heat, swelling, and pain. The signs were first described by Celsius, a Roman physician in the first century A.D. as rubor (redness), calor (heat), tumor (swelling), and dolor (pain). Galen, a Greek physician born in A.D. 130 in Pergamum who practiced in Rome, later defined inflammation as the body's reaction against injury. These signs are localized to the area of injury or infection and are most readily noted when the inflammation is on the body surface. Not all of these signs are present in every person with inflammation. In addition, a person with a major inflammation may develop a fever as well as malaise, anorexia (appetite loss), and nausea. For example, tuberculosis causes major inflammation of the lung and other tissues. Victims become anorexic and lose a lot of weight, which is why the disease has also been called "consumption." Figure 4.1 shows an example of the cut surfaces of a normal liver.

INFLAMMATION AND HEALING

Inflammation in response to infection begins when white blood cells recognize an invading virus or bacterium and release

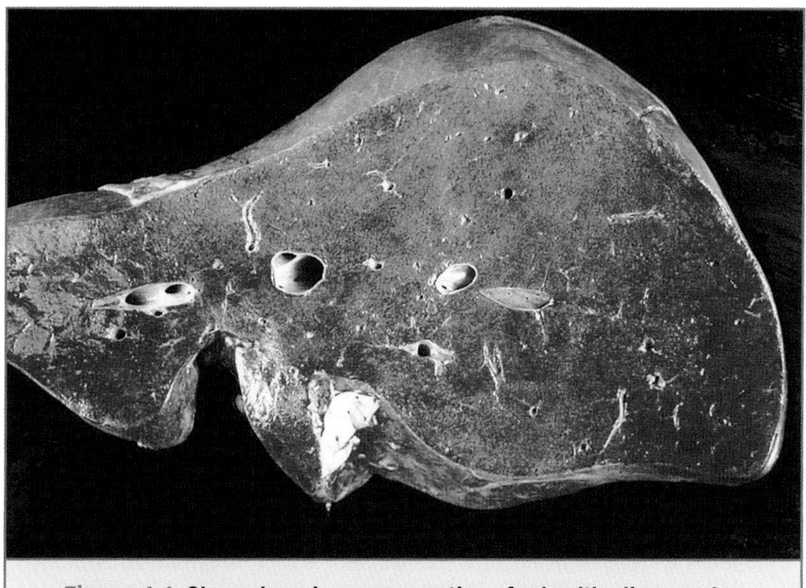

Figure 4.1 **Shown here is a cross section of a healthy liver made with a sharp knife. This is how the liver would appear without the aid of magnification. Some large blood vessels can be seen. Note the fine texture of the red-brown liver tissue. (University of Alabama, Department of Pathology)**

chemicals (cytokines) that alert other immune system cells that an invader is present. Then, a very complicated cascade of events follows. Blood flow increases to the site of infection. This is mediated by the release of histamine by specialized white blood cells known as basophils. The histamine causes dilation of the localized blood vessels (vasodilation) thus allowing a greater flow of blood to the area. This allows more immune cells to reach the site to fight the infection, and the blood delivers more nutrients and oxygen to the tissue cells to provide for increased metabolism and oxygen burning. One result of this is that the tissue becomes warmer or heats up. The blood vessels leak water, white blood cells, and proteins. This causes swelling and gives white blood cells and immune system proteins easier access to infected sites to attack the invader in the tissues. Meanwhile, the inflammatory chemicals irritate nerve endings in the tissue, which causes pain. This is brought about particularly by a chemical called bradykinin, which is also secreted by basophils. It, too, acts to dilate blood vessels.

Healing of tissue damage during inflammation proceeds through three processes, and healing begins almost as soon as inflammation begins. The healing actually competes with the inflammation. If the cause of inflammation cannot be removed, then the healing processes may produce abnormal or nonfunctional tissues. This is often the case in chronic hepatitis when cirrhosis develops.

The resolution process of healing occurs early when there is little tissue damage. Specialized cells called **macrophages** enter the inflamed area from the blood and scavenge (eat) dead cells and any other debris created by the injury or infection, such as pus, using a process called phagocytosis. The original structure of the tissue is left intact. If the immune system defeats the invading microbe, the tissue is restored to normal.

The regeneration process of healing occurs when lost cells are replaced by **proliferation** (division and growth) of cells of the same kind. Liver hepatocytes are most capable of this response, although other tissues like skin and bones have a limited ability to regenerate small losses. The key to a successful regeneration is to accurately reproduce the structure of the damaged tissue. This is easy with a simple tissue like the skin, but it is very difficult for a complex organ like the liver. Imperfect regeneration may occur in the liver because only the hepatocytes proliferate easily. Other cells that contribute to the structure of the liver do not reproduce as well.

Extensive or ongoing damage to the liver structure can result in cirrhosis, a condition of abnormal tissue structure and abnormal function. Hepatocytes proliferate but cannot assemble into the normal lobular structure. Instead, they form small balls or nodules that are isolated from the blood because new blood vessels do not develop normally and scarring obstructs them. An example of a liver with severe cirrhosis is shown in Figure 4.2. Ongoing liver damage can occur with chronic infections, including some forms of viral hepatitis (Figure 4.3), or with chronic exposure to toxic chemicals such as alcohol. Cirrhosis is not reversible, but its progress can be stopped in

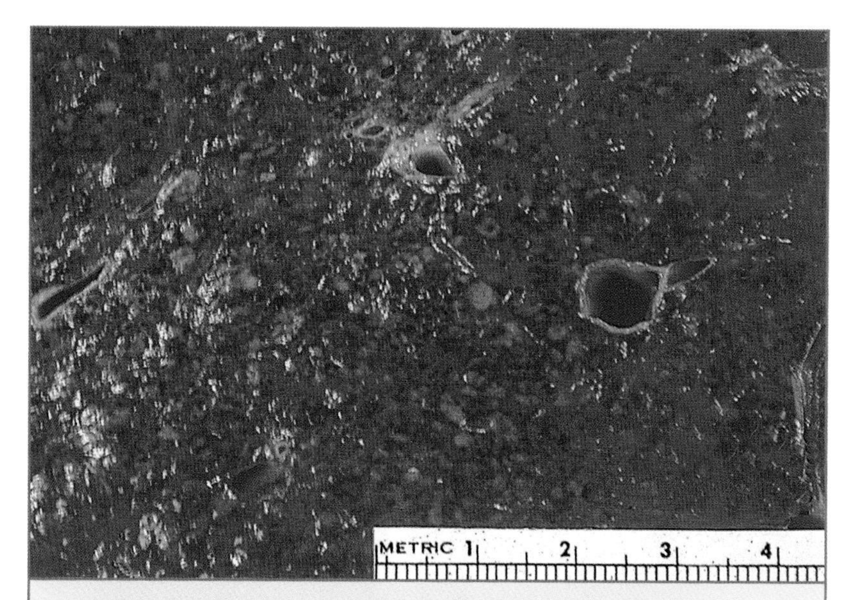

Figure 4.2 **This is a cross section made with a sharp knife of a liver with advanced cirrhosis. The image has been magnified about three times. Some large blood vessels can be seen. Obstructed blood flow due to scarring occurs at the level of the capillaries and lobules, which are not visible in this view. Compare the coarse texture of this tissue with the normal texture of the liver in Figure 4.1. Note that many balls, or nodules, which are about 3 to 5 mm in diameter, have a yellow color where liver cells have proliferated abnormally around scar tissue. Often the nodules will fuse to form larger nodules up to 5 cm in diameter. The nodules have a very poor blood supply and most of this tissue is not functional. (University of Alabama, Department of Pathology)**

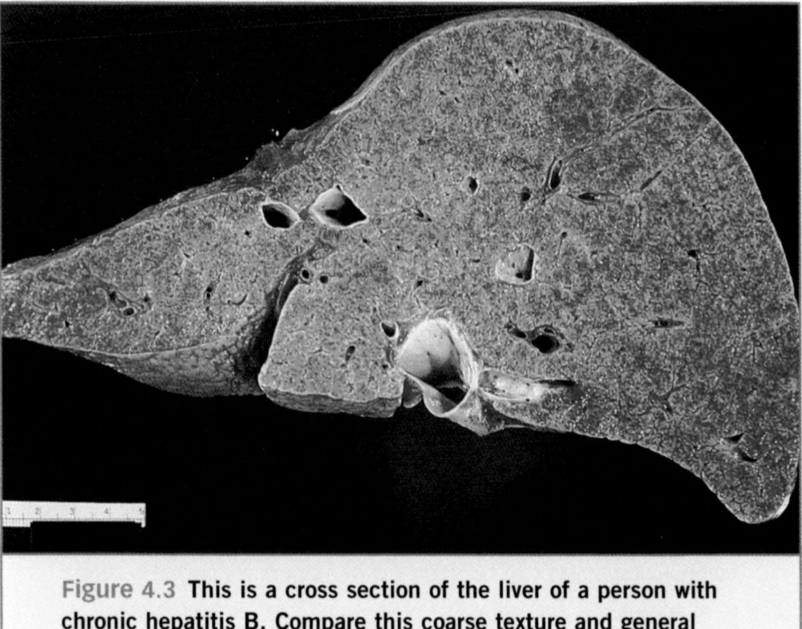

Figure 4.3 **This is a cross section of the liver of a person with chronic hepatitis B. Compare this coarse texture and general yellow appearance with the texture and color of the normal liver in Figure 4.1. The nodules built up around scar tissue are extensive. Some nodules are about 1 cm in diameter. This is an example of a liver at the end stage of the disease. (University of Alabama, Department of Pathology)**

some cases. However, it ultimately causes death if it proceeds for very long.

The repair process of healing results in the formation of scars. Fibroblasts are specialized cells present in all tissues that produce the structural network or meshwork of fibers in a tissue that connects or holds all the other cells together. This network is called connective tissue and consists of many different proteins, including the most abundant one, collagen. When extensive tissue loss has happened and regeneration is slow or not occurring at all, fibroblasts migrate to the damaged area and produce collagen to fill the void. The collagen ultimately becomes a scar.

KILLER T CELLS AND APOPTOSIS

Killer T cells, also known as cytotoxic T cells, are activated by helper T cells that give them a modified copy of an antigen's epitope. An infected cell may succeed in getting a copy of an epitope from the microbe once it is inside the cell. The cell can then attach this epitope to the external surface of its own cell membrane, where an activated killer T cell can recognize and bind to it. Once binding occurs, a series of changes is triggered in the T cell, causing a specific kind of attack on the infected cell that leads to the death of the cell by apoptosis (a pattern of cell death). It can be said that the T cell induces the suicide of the target cell because all destructive effects are produced by the target cell itself. Cell death by apoptosis is also known as programmed cell death because it occurs in an orderly, well-defined manner. Apoptosis can be triggered in many ways and also serves to eliminate old and defective cells when there is no infection.

During apoptosis, a cascade of chemical reactions begins in the infected cell, which leads to the activation of a group of enzymes known as caspases (*c*ysteine-dependent *as*partate-directed prot*eases*). Some caspases destroy proteins that make

IMMUNE RESPONSE

The immune response has **humoral** (pertaining to body fluids) and cellular parts. The **humoral response** involves antibodies that are produced by a special class of white blood cells called B lymphocytes (**B cells**). Antibodies are also called **immunoglobulins**, abbreviated Ig. They are proteins that interact specifically with a foreign substance or antigen. They actually react with a small part of the antigen called an **epitope**. The antibodies are released by the B cells and circulate in the blood separately or bound to the surface of white blood cells. There are five classes of immunoglobulins: IgG, IgM, IgA, IgD, and IgE. IgG and IgM make up 93% of the antibodies found in human blood. IgM antibodies are usually the first to be produced in response to an

up the structural skeleton of the cell, others destroy proteins in the cell nucleus that are essential for gene function, and others activate enzymes that destroy the cell's DNA. Some caspases can also destroy the DNA or RNA of an infecting microbe, thus killing it within the cell. These destructive events do not cause the cell to just disintegrate and release all of its contents to the surrounding tissue, as in the process known as lysis. With apoptosis, the cell ultimately breaks up into fragments that enclose cell contents, including the infecting agent. These fragments are then taken up by macrophages that devour and destroy them completely. The killer T cells are not destroyed in this process. After they have initiated apoptosis in one cell, they can detach and look for other infected cells.

After the killer T cells have done their job and all of the infecting agent has been destroyed, the immune response must be terminated, or else the T cells will begin to attack healthy cells. Termination occurs when the T cells bind to each other and, for lack of a better target, initiate apoptosis in each other. Apoptotic cell debris is then cleaned up by macrophages.

antigen, followed by the IgG antibodies, which usually remain in the blood after an infection is over and provide immunity against reinfection.

Antibodies are Y-shaped proteins produced by B cells. Antigens are proteins with small structural parts called epitopes that are unique to the foreign invader. The B cell modifies part of the basic antibody protein to a structure that is complementary to the antigen epitope so that parts of the antigen and antibody can fit together like a lock and key (Figure 4.4).

Antibodies work in one of three specific ways. In the first, they may bind to the antigens on the surface of a bacterium or virus and make that invader recognizable by a special class

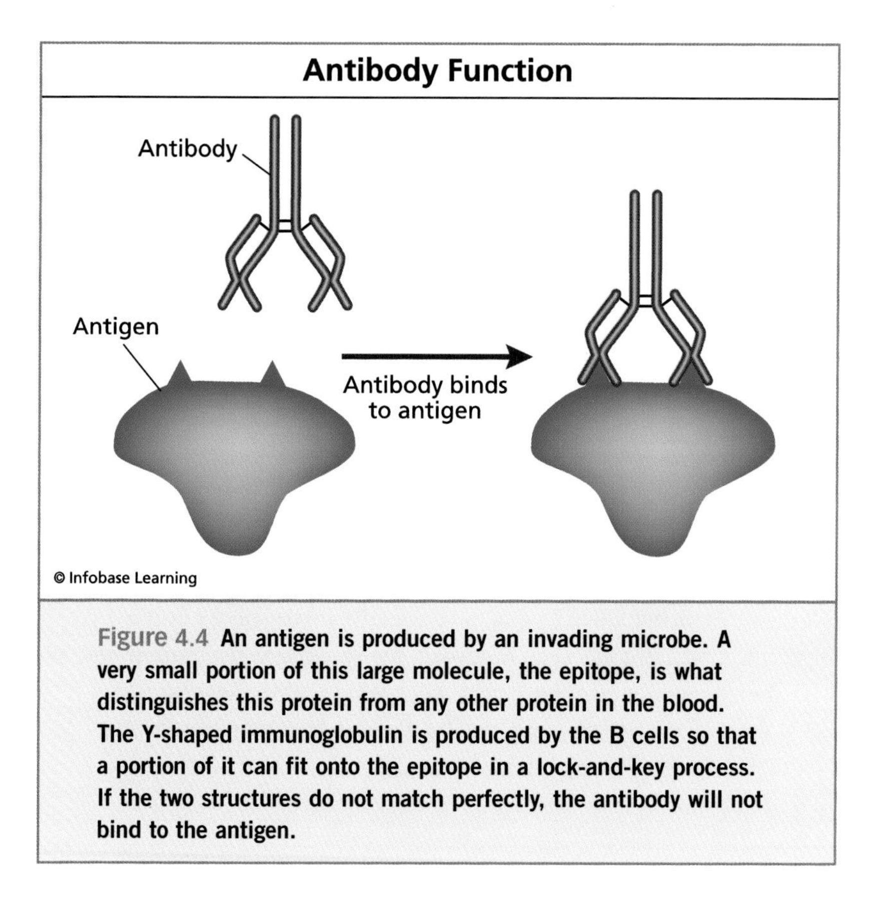

Figure 4.4 **An antigen is produced by an invading microbe. A very small portion of this large molecule, the epitope, is what distinguishes this protein from any other protein in the blood. The Y-shaped immunoglobulin is produced by the B cells so that a portion of it can fit onto the epitope in a lock-and-key process. If the two structures do not match perfectly, the antibody will not bind to the antigen.**

of cells called **phagocytes** that then engulf and destroy the invader through a process called **phagocytosis**. A second kind of antibody binds to the antigens on the surface of a virus and prevents the virus from entering cells. This blocks the infection because viruses must enter cells to reproduce. Viruses do not have reproductive machinery of their own and must "hijack" the reproductive machinery of the cells they infect. After binding to antigen, the third kind of antibodies then react with substances produced by the liver called **complement proteins**. This interaction results in the opening up of the cell membrane of the bacterium or the infected cell and the destruction of the target by an explosion-like process known as lysis. Macrophages then clean up the mess.

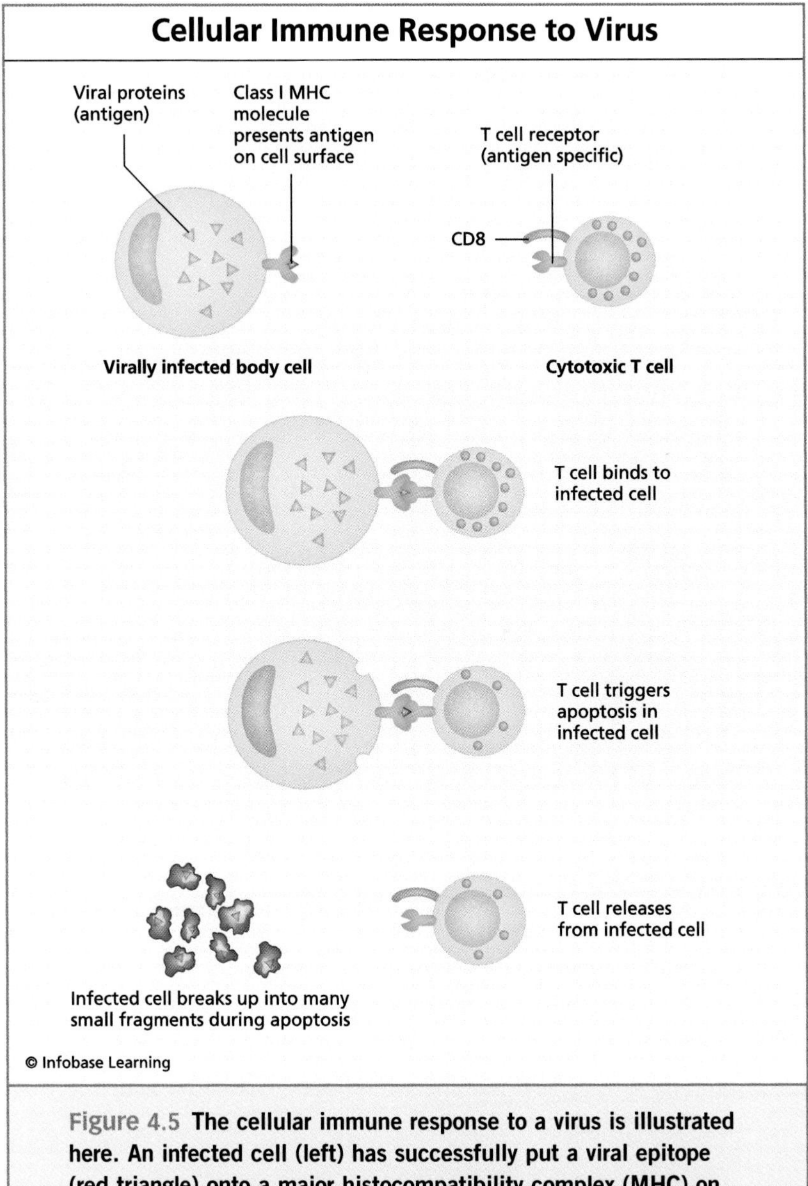

Figure 4.5 The cellular immune response to a virus is illustrated here. An infected cell (left) has successfully put a viral epitope (red triangle) onto a major histocompatibility complex (MHC) on its surface. A killer T cell (right), also known as a CD8+ cytotoxic T cell, has been activated and given a complementary copy of the epitope to recognize and bind to it at the MHC. Binding triggers apoptosis in the infected cell, destroying its internal structure and breaking it up into many dense, membrane-enclosed particles that also contain the viruses. The killer T cell is not affected, and is free to attack other infected cells.

The cellular response involves another special class of white blood cells, called **T lymphocytes** because the cells migrate from the bone marrow to the thymus gland in order to mature. The thymus is a small gland located high in the chest behind the breastbone. There are two kinds of T cells: helper T cells and killer T cells. Helper T cells are the guardians or patrolmen of the body. They are the first to recognize an antigen. Next, they alert the B cells (see Figure 4.5) and give them the epitope template to make specific antibodies against the invader. They then coordinate the overall immune response. Helper T cells also activate the killer T cells and give them a processed copy of the antigen epitope. The killer T cells are the enforcers. They use the epitope information to identify, attack, and destroy diseased cells. Infected cells can take an epitope from the invading microbe and attach it to the cell surface, where activated killer T cells can recognize it. The epitope attachment occurs by way of a cell membrane protein known as a **major histocompatibility complex (MHC)**. Killer T cells attack the diseased cells, not the foreign body, and are very important for fighting viral infections. Destruction of an infected cell also eliminates the viruses in that cell. Both B and T lymphocytes circulate within the blood, on guard for foreign invaders, but they must be activated by the helper T cells to do their job.

When a person is initially infected with a hepatitis virus, the immune system attempts to respond and eliminate the virus—a typical response to any virus or other microbe. But the immune system also has special features that depend on the nature of the virus.

5

The Story of Viruses

It was the 1860s and the French wine industry was facing a major problem when its wines were turning to vinegar. They implored the famous Louis Pasteur to help them save the industry from ruin. After all, he had a reputation for being one of the most knowledgeable scientists of his day and also for understanding a great deal about microbiology.

Pasteur looked at the wine under his microscope and discovered that it contained rod-shaped bacteria as well as the round yeast that should have been there for the fermentation process. He used filters to clear out the bacteria and the wine was saved, not to mention France's biggest industry. This success helped to establish the germ theory of disease.

However, it was found that some diseases were caused by an agent that was present when bacteria were not. These agents could not be filtered out like bacteria could. In 1885, Pasteur saved the life of nine-year-old Joseph Meister, who had been bitten by a rabid dog. He would be doomed to certain death if Pasteur did not administer a vaccine he had created using one of these agents. The boy was saved and lived another 55 years.

Thanks to the work of Dmitri Ivanovsky and Martinus Beijerinck with tobacco plants, the causative agent of a disease that was destroying them was discovered. Although it could not be seen with a microscope as bacteria could, it was named Tobacco Mosaic Virus. Their work, done in the 1890s, was the beginning of the study of virology. In the 1930s, filters were invented that could filter out particles as small as viruses and the first electron microscope was invented. These two inventions led to the actual visualization of viruses.

Some important background information about viruses is needed to understand the specific hepatitis viruses.

Viruses are among the smallest biological things we know of. At one time, viruses were considered the smallest, but a smaller group of infectious objects called prions has been found. Prions are neither bacterial, fungal, nor viral, but are proteins that normally occur in a harmless form. For reasons that are not clear, the once harmless protein folds into an aberrant form that makes it cause disease. In addition to this, it is able to cause other harmless prions to fold into harmful shapes as well. Prions have been blamed for causing several neurological diseases, including Creutzfeldt-Jakob disease, scrapie (a disease of sheep and goats), kuru (a progressive fatal brain disease transmitted by cannibalism in New Guinea), mad cow disease, and possibly some forms of Alzheimer's disease. The picornaviruses are among the smallest viruses and measure 25 to 35 nanometers in diameter. This is extremely small. One nanometer is about 40 billionths of an inch. This family of very small viruses includes those that cause poliomyelitis, the common cold, and hepatitis A. Viruses are 10 to 100 times smaller than bacteria and up to 100,000 times smaller than the head of a pin. They are not visible with a standard light microscope, but can be viewed with an electron microscope. Electron microscopes can magnify objects by up to 1 million times their size, or about 200 times more than the best light microscopes. The first image of a virus was obtained only after the electron microscope was developed in the 1930s.

More than 400 different viruses that infect humans are known. Viruses have existed about as long as life itself, although they probably could not develop before the very first cells did because they need cells to reproduce.

VIRAL REPLICATION

Viruses replicate (reproduce) in five steps: (1) The virus attaches to a host cell; (2) it penetrates the host; (3) viral nucleic acid is released into the host, where it initiates and guides the production or synthesis of new viral protein and **nucleic acid** using the machinery of the host cell; (4) new viruses, made up of newly synthesized viral nucleic acid and proteins, are assembled with the help of other proteins that are coded by viral nucleic acid and synthesized by the infected cell; and (5) the new viruses leave the host to search for new hosts. Viruses are pure parasites. They cannot live independently. They are able to reproduce and function only inside a host cell, and they use the energy normally available to the host for its own reproductive functions. Each virus has unique details for its replication, but all conform to this general format.

An active virus essentially hijacks the host cell's metabolic machinery for its own purposes. The metabolic machinery of a cell is composed of all the vital chemical reactions that are required to keep the cell alive and to perform its special functions. The consequence of this hijacking is that the host cell is less able to meet its own needs or the needs of other cells in the body that depend on it. Cells may die and the whole organism may develop symptoms that are caused by the loss of important cell functions. An infected person feels sick for these reasons and because the immune response to the virus can cause symptoms such as inflammation and fever.

Viruses have relatively simple structures. They consist of a nucleic acid (the viral genome), which can be either DNA or RNA, and one or a few proteins. One criterion for classifying viruses is whether they have DNA or RNA. Viral nucleic acid usually has only a few genes, perhaps 20 or fewer, which are needed to ensure the reproduction of the virus. The nucleic

DNA AND THE GENETIC CODE

There are two kinds of nucleic acid that are named for the molecular subunits or building blocks that make up their backbones. The building block deoxyribose, which is a kind of sugar molecule, is found in deoxyribonucleic acid, or DNA. DNA is always present in the cell nucleus in animals and contains all the genes that define what an animal is. It is a huge molecule that is usually twisted into a helix like a screw. In animals, two strands of the helix are twisted together into a double helix that looks rather like two strings of beads that have been twisted together.

Attached to each deoxyribose is one of four molecules. Two of these molecules are called purines, named adenine (A) and guanine (G). The other two molecules are called pyrimidines and named thymine (T) and cytosine (C). These molecules have a chemical property that classifies them as bases. They also like to link up loosely with each other using hydrogen bonds to form base pairs in a very specific manner. They never link up with the other bases. Thus, we get the pairs A–T and C–G, and no others. When an adenine on one DNA strand is opposite a thymine on the other strand, the two link up. The same thing happens between cytosine and guanine. In fact, the two strands are synthesized to be complementary so that opposite bases always link up.

On the other side of the deoxyribose sugar is a phosphate group. A string of these groups makes up the backbone of one strand of the DNA double helix molecule. The combination of the phosphate group, the deoxyribose sugar, and the base is called a nucleotide. The nucleotides of both strands of the DNA molecule link together at their bases to hold the DNA together.

The sequence of bases in one strand of the DNA defines the genetic code. A set of three successive bases is called a codon and defines a single amino acid. For example, the codon TTC defines the amino acid phenylalanine and the codon ACG defines the amino acid threonine.

acid may be a single strand or a double strand. How many strands it has is another way to classify viruses.

The nucleic acid in a virus is enclosed by a protein coat known as a **capsid**, which helps protect the nucleic acid from attack by enzymes. It contains special sites that allow it to recognize and attach to a host cell and other sites that allow it to penetrate the host cell membrane and enter the cell. Many viruses have spikes of protein that make the capsid look like a pincushion. These spikes extend out from the capsid surface and contain the host-recognition sites that allow the virus to bind to the surface of a host cell. Remarkably, the capsids of some viruses consist of a single kind of protein. Other capsids have 10 different proteins. The capsid is made up of many protein subunits called **capsomers**. About 150 to 200 capsomers are assembled into the final capsid structure around the nucleic acid during reproduction of the virus.

The capsid-enclosed nucleic acid is called a **nucleocapsid**. Sometimes the nucleocapsid makes up the complete virus. The shape of the capsid depends on the general shape of the nucleic acid. If the nucleic acid is like an extended, thick, twisted string or rope, it will form a screw-like structure called a helix. The capsomers assemble around this extended string to form a cylinder or rod-shaped nucleocapsid. Viruses with this structure are referred to as helical viruses because of the helical twist of the nucleic acid, and the nucleic acid is usually single-stranded RNA—probably the simplest form of a virus. If the nucleic acid string is balled up rather than extended, then the capsid forms a 20-sided polygon to enclose the ball, called an **icosahedron**, whose sides are equilateral triangles. The icosahedron looks like a sphere because it has so many sides, and this form of nucleocapsid is often called spherical. Another criterion for classifying a virus is its helical or spherical structure. Spherical viruses are the most common, and all hepatitis viruses are spherical.

RNA AND PROTEIN SYNTHESIS

The building block ribose, another sugar molecule that is similar to deoxyribose, but has one more oxygen atom, makes up ribonucleic acid, or RNA. RNA occurs in three important and different forms. All forms of RNA are produced in the cell nucleus but move out into the cytoplasm, where they perform their functions. Messenger RNA (mRNA) contains all the codons in the proper sequence needed to produce a single protein from the amino acid building blocks of proteins. It acquires this information from the gene for the protein in a process called transcription. mRNA is also a large molecule, though not as large as DNA. The larger the protein to be built, the larger the mRNA. mRNA is moved from the nucleus into the cytoplasm, where protein synthesis occurs on the ribosomes.

Within the cytoplasm is a second form of RNA known as transfer RNA, or tRNA. It is much smaller than mRNA and has a special function. There is one kind of tRNA for each of the 20 different amino acids that can be in a protein. Each tRNA

A single capsomer protein may perform multiple functions for the virus because it is usually very large and can have many functional zones along its length. The nucleocapsid of some viruses is enclosed by a membrane called the **envelope**. This membrane is derived from the host cell membrane as the virus exits the host cell in a process called **budding**. Budding occurs when a virus pushes outward on the cell membrane and the membrane folds around the capsid until finally the membrane breaks free of the cell and closes up with the virus inside. However, the virus always inserts some of its own proteins from the capsid into the envelope. These serve to attach and bind the virus to other host cells, which are like the spike proteins described above. The presence or absence of an envelope is yet another criterion for classifying a virus. Budding does not necessarily kill the host cell.

recognizes one amino acid and can grab onto or bind it. The tRNA serves to transfer the amino acid from the cytoplasm into the protein-synthesizing complex known as the ribosome.

The third form of RNA is ribosomal RNA (rRNA). It is coiled up and is a crucial part of the ribosome. Ribosomes are attached to the surface of membrane-enclosed sacks called the endoplasmic reticulum, or ER. mRNA binds to a ribosome and the rRNA interprets the codon sequence in the mRNA for making a protein. The tRNA binds to the rRNA to deliver the specific amino acid called for by a codon on the mRNA. The mRNA slides through the rRNA from one end to the other. At each codon, a tRNA delivers the amino acid called for and detaches from the ribosome, the amino acid is incorporated into the growing protein molecule, and the rRNA shifts to read another codon. The newly synthesized protein may be released into the cell cytoplasm or into the interior of the ER, where it may undergo additional changes before it is released to the cytoplasm as a fully functional protein.

Not all viruses exit the host cell by budding. Others release enzymes that bore holes in the cell membrane that cause the membrane to rupture, or lyse, thereby liberating the virus in the form of a nucleocapsid. The complete virus structure that exits a host cell and can infect other cells is referred to as a **virion**.

TESTING FOR VIRUSES

Testing for a virus can be done by several methods. The following are those used routinely by medical laboratories for detection of the hepatitis viruses.

Radioimmunoassay and Immunofluorescence

A blood sample is treated with an antibody that is labeled either with a radioactive material in a radioimmunoassay (RIA), or with a molecule that glows when a light shines on it, in an immunofluorescence assay. If an antigen is present, the antibody binds to it and the complex can be detected by sensitive measuring techniques.

ELISA

A second method of establishing that a virus infection is present is the detection of specific antibodies in the blood. This approach cannot establish that there is still live virus because the immune system ensures that some antibody is always present even after a virus has been successfully eliminated. This provides immunity to reinfection by the same microbe. Furthermore, the immune system may not yet have produced antibody at the time of the test if the infection was very recent.

An enzyme-linked immunosorbent assay (ELISA) is used most frequently (Figure 5.1). A glass plate is prepared that has many shallow wells bored into it. A known antigen from a specific virus is attached to the surface of the glass walls in the wells. Blood serum is applied to the wells and then washed off after a while. If antibody is present in the serum, it will bind to the antigen on the glass and stay there. A second antibody, prepared in the laboratory and known to bind to all human antibodies, is then applied to the well. If viral antibody is present, the secondary antibody will bind to it. The secondary antibody has an enzyme attached (linked) to it that can react with certain chemicals called chromogens and change their colors. The secondary antibody is washed off after a while and a chromogen solution is applied. Finally, the well is inspected for color to determine whether an antibody has been found. The intensity of the color is related directly to the amount of antibody in the sample, so it is also possible to measure the concentration of antibody in the blood.

A simple ELISA test may not be sensitive enough to detect some viruses, such as the hepatitis C virus. A second-generation enzyme immunoassay, EIA-2, was developed in 1992. It is much

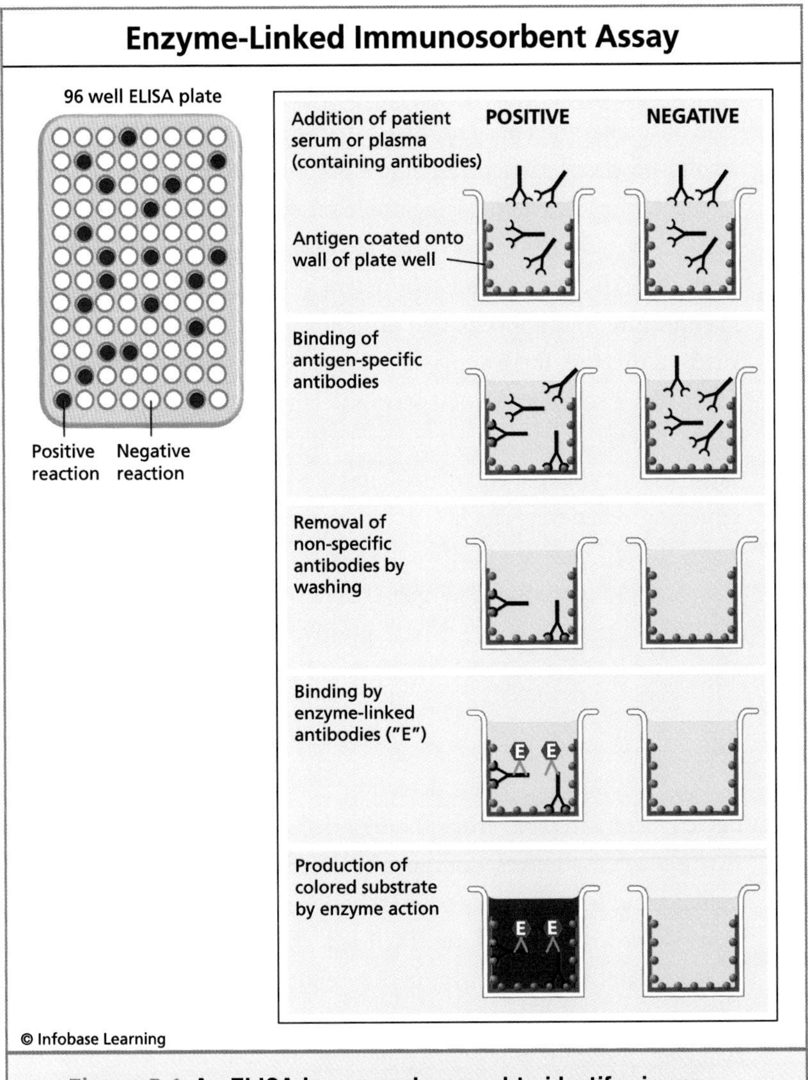

Figure 5.1 An ELISA is a procedure used to identify viruses. The glass plate used for this test has 96 wells. Each well may be coated with one antigen specific for the virus for which the doctors are looking, or groups of wells may each have a different antigen. Patient serum is added to each well, and the procedure occurs as shown. If a specific antibody is present in serum, it will cause a color change in the wells that contain the correct antigen.

more sensitive than ELISA and has enabled routine screening of donated blood for hepatitis C virus. This test is done much like an ELISA, except that several viral antigens are used rather than just one antigen. The EIA-2 test can give false-positive results, however, particularly at low antibody titers.

Another test, called a recombinant immunoblot assay, or RIBA-2, was developed to check for false-positive results with the EIA-2. The term *recombinant* refers to the technique used to manufacture four antigens that are known to be present in the virus. In this test, these antigens are attached to a strip of special paper and a sample of blood serum is blotted onto the strip. If antibodies are present, they bind to the antigens on the strip and cause a color change. The RIBA-2 test is used routinely in blood screening whenever the EIA-2 test is positive for hepatitis C virus. If both tests are positive, it is concluded that hepatitis C virus antibodies are in the sample. If the EIA-2 test is positive and the RIBA-2 test is negative, a false-positive test result has probably occurred. A second blood sample and retesting may be done.

PCR

A third method of virus detection is to measure the viral nucleic acid extracted from the blood. The polymerase chain reaction (PCR) makes this possible. PCR is a very sensitive method and is useful only when the infection is active and live virus is present in the blood. PCR is a chemical reaction produced by a polymerase enzyme that replicates the viral nucleic acid as long as there are bases or nucleic acid building blocks available. Building blocks and enzymes are added to a serum sample. A reaction starts if there is any nucleic acid present at all and it just keeps going until all building blocks are used up. However, PCR is expensive to perform and is not used as routinely as other methods. Furthermore, medical scientists have not agreed upon standards for doing the test and the Food and Drug Administration has approved it only for screening for active infections of some viruses, such as hepatitis C virus.

6

Hepatitis A

Rhonda was a high school senior who enjoyed eating fresh fruits and vegetables. One day she went out for lunch with some friends to a popular restaurant known for its all-you-can-eat salad bar. Rhonda took advantage of the salad bar and impressed her friends with how much salad she could eat. Everyone had a good time, and Rhonda's reputation was sealed as the premier salad-cruncher in town.

Three weeks after the lunch party, Rhonda became ill. First, she felt very tired and had a mild fever. It wasn't flu season, but she thought she might have picked up some kind of bug. She rested for a day but did not get better. In fact, she became nauseated, had pain in her abdomen, and began to vomit. Her mother made an appointment for her to see the doctor the next day. On the day of her appointment, Rhonda noticed that her urine had turned very dark yellow. The doctor examined Rhonda and decided to do a blood test to screen for microbe infections. He suspected viral hepatitis because Rhonda's symptoms were a textbook example of acute hepatitis symptoms. He also knew from her medical history that Rhonda had not been vaccinated for hepatitis A or B. He advised Rhonda to rest at home and be patient while he waited for the test results.

The next day, the whites of Rhonda's eyes yellowed. She had jaundice; she was in the icteric phase of a hepatitis infection. Her fever and other symptoms, except fatigue, were not as bad. She actually began to feel better, but still had jaundice and was fatigued. The doctor called a day later and said that Rhonda's test result for hepatitis A was positive. In other words, her blood level of the antibody for the hepatitis A virus, IgM-A, was high. This was a good sign because it meant her immune system was fighting the infection and would ultimately eliminate the virus. She was told that her symptoms should subside within a few weeks and that she should recover completely in a month or two. The jaundice might get worse for the next week or so, but then would clear up as she recovered. She would have to avoid strenuous activity and get plenty of rest, but she could resume most of her activities as soon as she felt well enough. She would then be immune to future hepatitis A infections for the rest of her life.

The doctor also advised Rhonda and her family not to share eating utensils or drinking glasses. Rhonda must wash her hands frequently, especially after a bowel movement, and should not help with food preparation or dishwashing until after she was fully recovered. Rhonda was delighted with that last piece of advice! The doctor wanted Rhonda to make weekly office visits until she had recovered so he could track the progress of the disease. There was a very slight chance that the infection could trigger fulminant hepatitis, and the doctor wanted to be on the lookout for it.

The source of Rhonda's infection was a mystery to everyone. The doctor reported Rhonda's infection to the public health authorities. This is a routine procedure for all hepatitis infections and certain other communicable diseases. Public health authorities do not need to know the names of patients, but they need to know about communicable infections to determine whether a disease **outbreak** *(sudden increase of a disease in a small area) is in progress. Such knowledge enables them to take steps to curb the outbreak and protect the public health. The authorities observed that within the past month, they had received reports of 110 hepatitis A infections in the county where Rhonda lives. Two of the people, who were elderly, died from fulminant hepatitis. All of the surviving victims recovered fully. The health officials noted that four of the infected people worked as waitresses in the same restaurant that Rhonda had visited. A little more investigation revealed that all of the victims had eaten there. This was considered an outbreak. Health inspectors visited the restaurant and encouraged the employees to have blood tests. The restaurant closed* *until further notice. One restaurant employee, a dishwasher, was found to have had a hepatitis A infection, although he had not suffered any symptoms. The restaurant did a thorough cleaning of the kitchen and all of its dishes, silverware, and cooking utensils with a strong bleach solution before it reopened.*

HEPATITIS A VIRUS

Hepatitis A virus, abbreviated HAV, is among the smallest of viruses. It belongs to the family of picornaviruses, which includes the poliovirus and the rhinoviruses that cause the common cold. The virus has an icosahedron (20-sided)-shaped capsid. The capsid is made up of 60 capsomers, which are composed of four different proteins. Three of the proteins are exposed on the surface of the capsid and contain the binding sites that allow the virus to attach to and enter a host cell. The nucleic acid is single-stranded RNA. It has is no envelope.

The most important immune response to HAV is cellular rather than humoral (pertaining to body fluids). Killer T cells are activated that attack and destroy infected hepatocytes by inducing apoptosis (programmed cell death). In most cases, the process does not go on long enough to cause major damage to the liver, and hepatocytes regenerate once the virus is gone. B cells, activated by the helper T cells, help activate the killer T cells and produce the immunoglobulin IgM-A. There is a significant amount of virus in the blood during the acute phase of the infection, and IgM-A attacks that virus directly. However, most of the virus is found inside the hepatocytes or shed in the feces. IgM-A serves as an important marker for an acute HAV infection and is looked for in blood tests. Its level in the blood reaches a peak about six weeks after infection and then fades away. However, a second antibody, IgG-A, is produced more slowly by the B cells. This antibody reaches a high level in the blood two months after infection and remains there for a very long time. It is IgG-A that can provide a defense against future infections by HAV by attacking the virus directly as it enters the blood and before it can enter the hepatocytes. IgG-A in the blood with no IgM-A is proof that a person has been immunized against hepatitis A, either through a self-limited infection (as with the dishwasher at the restaurant) or a vaccine.

The virus reproduces in the general way described in Chapter 5. Once the virus enters the cell, it releases its nucleic acid into the **cytoplasm**. The viral RNA takes control of the cell's nucleic acid and protein synthesis systems to produce more viral RNA and capsid proteins (Figure 6.1). Capsomers assemble into capsids that enclose a single viral RNA. The capsids are then enclosed within a small membranous vesicle (like a bubble) that can fuse with the hepatocyte membrane only at sites next to bile canaliculi. The vesicles fuse, open up to the outside, and release virus to the bile. This process does not kill the hepatocytes; rather, it is the killer T cells that do so. Once in the bile, the new viruses can infect neighboring hepatocytes or make their way to the gut, where some re-enter the blood and the rest are shed in the feces.

TRANSMISSION OF HAV

People with active virus infections but without symptoms are called **carriers**. Trillions of viruses can be present in a carrier. A person may acquire an HAV infection by contact with infected feces or with objects that have come in contact with infected feces, followed by ingestion of the virus. Only 10 to 100 viruses need to be ingested to establish an infection.

HAV is an enteric virus. The ingested virus crosses the gut wall, enters the blood, finds its way to the liver, and infects hepatocytes. Feces-contaminated water is the principal route of transmission of HAV. Carriers who are careless about hand-washing may pass the virus on to others. Other ways of acquiring an infection include eating fresh foods that have been handled by a carrier or washed with contaminated water; using eating utensils that have been handled by a carrier; changing the diaper of an infected infant or touching a diaper-changing

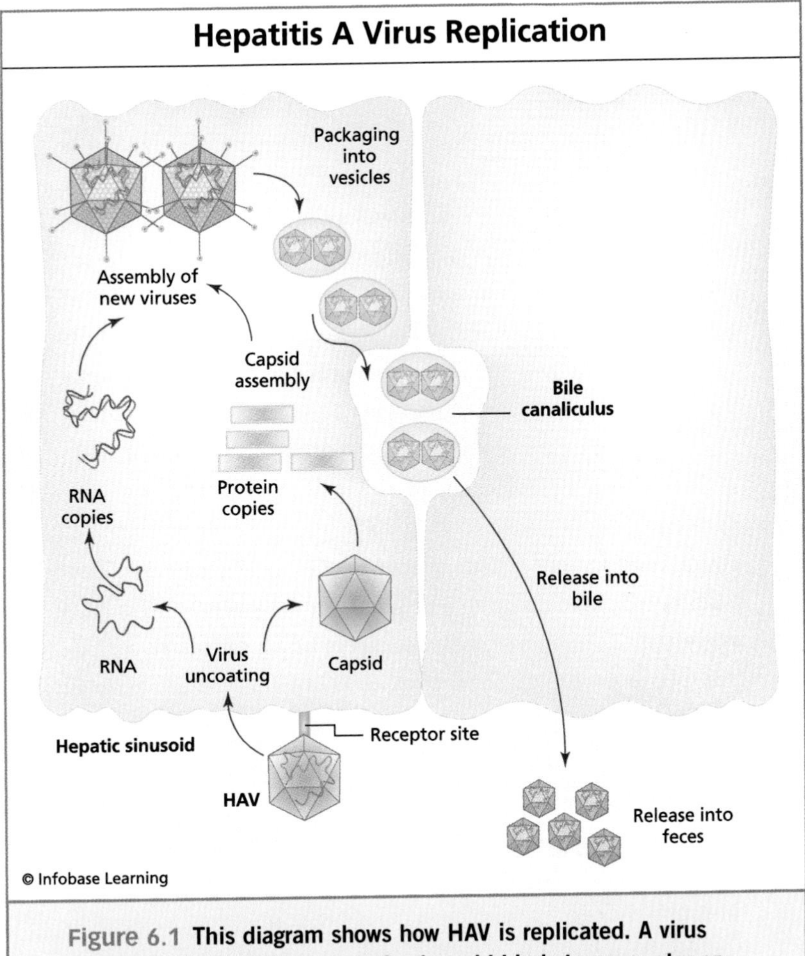

Figure 6.1 This diagram shows how HAV is replicated. A virus present in the blood in a hepatic sinusoid binds to a receptor on the hepatocyte membrane, thereby gaining entry into the cell. Within the cell, the capsid is released and the viral RNA enters the cell cytoplasm. Viral RNA and proteins are reproduced by the cell metabolic systems and new virions are assembled. Virions are packaged in vesicles for release into the bile canaliculi, from which they either enter other hepatocytes, flow to the gut for excretion, or go back into the blood.

table that has not been well cleaned and then not washing one's hands before eating; sharing eating utensils or food handled by a family member who is a carrier; and eating raw shellfish harvested from or washed with contaminated water. Rhonda probably ingested HAV by eating with contaminated utensils in the restaurant.

The older a person is, the more likely it is that HAV will cause symptoms. Infants and young children rarely suffer symptoms, so parents have no way of knowing that a child is ill. Symptom-free carriers are likely to spread the disease. An estimated 90% of children in underdeveloped countries are infected early in life and do not suffer symptoms; therefore, most adults who were born and raised in such countries are immune to the disease. However, visitors from developed countries are at a very high risk for infection unless they have been immunized.

WHERE THE DISEASE OCCURS

Hepatitis A is a very serious disease worldwide. About 1.5 million cases are reported to the World Health Organization (WHO) every year. These cases cost in excess of an estimated $3 billion per year. About 30,000 to 50,000 of these cases arise in the United States, costing about $665 million per year. Experts estimate that 15 million new cases actually arise each year. The disease is misdiagnosed and underreported, probably because it often is symptom-free or causes minor flu-like symptoms, and because it is strictly an acute disease with a short duration. The **incidence** (number of new cases per year among a specified number of people) of the disease is very high in most underdeveloped countries with poor sanitation, water, and public health systems.

PREVENTION OF HAV

Good personal hygiene is one of the best ways to avoid HAV infection, as is being careful about the water you drink. Public health measures to protect the water supply can reduce the incidence of the disease dramatically. Public water in the United States is safe. Caution about foods is also appropriate. Avoid eating fresh fruits and vegetables and raw shellfish in

PUBLIC HEALTH AND CONSEQUENCES OF THE DISEASE

You may wonder why hepatitis A is considered a serious health problem in view of its mild or absent symptoms. Adults are more likely to suffer symptoms that are severe enough to prevent them from working for a few weeks or months, and adults older than 50 can be disabled for months or become seriously ill because of complications from other medical problems. Lost work in a developed country is usually a minor inconvenience because most people are protected by employer-provided sick leave. Lost work in an underdeveloped country can be very serious, however. Poor people have limited opportunities for work. Subsistence farmers could lose a harvest and an entire family could face starvation.

The high incidence of hepatitis A in underdeveloped countries is important for public health in the United States, Europe, and Japan. Many foodstuffs, especially fresh fruits and vegetables, are imported from underdeveloped countries. Produce may be handled by a hepatitis A virus carrier and washed with contaminated water before being shipped. Consumers in developed countries risk ingestion of contaminated food. For example, 600 people were infected by hepatitis A after eating contaminated onions at a single restaurant in Pennsylvania. The onions were imported from Mexico, where the incidence of hepatitis A is high.

underdeveloped countries unless you have been immunized. Anal intercourse should be avoided unless a condom is used or both partners have been immunized.

It is possible to receive temporary immunization from an injection of the immunoglobulin IgG-A. This protection lasts only as long as the IgG remains in the blood, which is about two to three months, because the B cells are not stimulated to

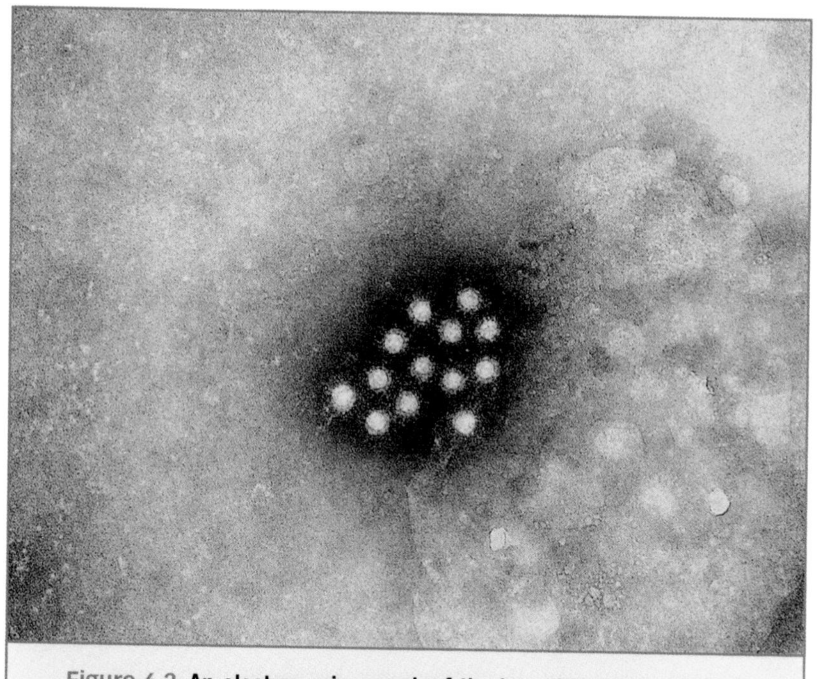

Figure 6.2 **An electron micrograph of the hepatitis A virus (HAV). This virus enters an organism by ingestion of water and food contaminated by human feces and reaches the liver through the bloodstream. (Centers for Disease Control and Prevention)**

produce the antibody. Stimulation of B cells can only be done by an HAV antigen. This approach works well to stop an acute infection when it is known that HAV exposure has occurred within the past two weeks. It is a useful preventive approach for a person planning to travel to areas with high disease incidence and remain for a short time. People who must depart on a trip quickly may not have time to develop immunity from a vaccination and may take advantage of IgG-A.

Permanent immunization with a vaccine lasts a lifetime. Vaccination is not recommended for all people in developed countries like the United States because the incidence of HAV is low and the cost per person for the vaccine is fairly high. The cost in the United States is about $42 per dose with complete vaccination requiring two immunizations six months apart. This cost is prohibitive in poor countries. In the United States, the Centers for Disease Control and Prevention (CDC) recommends that only a few groups of people be vaccinated. For instance, frequent travelers to areas of high HAV incidence should receive the vaccine. Food handlers, such as cafeteria and restaurant workers, should be vaccinated. Children who live in areas of the United States with a high HAV incidence, including poor rural areas and American Indian reservations, should be vaccinated. Men who have sex with men should also be vaccinated. Finally, intravenous (IV) drug users who share needles should be vaccinated because there is a small chance that live virus in the blood during the early phase of an HAV infection could be transmitted by way of a syringe needle.

7

Hepatitis B

Valerie, a young newlywed and six months pregnant, worked as a nurse at a large hospital. She scratched her finger early one morning while pruning a rosebush in her garden. She thought nothing of it and didn't bother to bandage the scratch. That afternoon, she went to work. A patient who had his blood drawn accidentally dropped on the floor the gauze pad that he used to press over the needle puncture site. Valerie quickly picked up the pad and put it in the medical waste bin. She wasn't wearing gloves at the time but thought she had been careful, and she washed her hands immediately afterward.

Three months later, Valerie gave birth to a beautiful baby boy, David. David had a healthy, normal childhood and grew up to be a strapping young man. One day David decided to donate blood in response to an urgent plea for donors from the local hospital. This was his first experience donating blood and he was nervous, but all went well and he left the hospital feeling good about helping others. About a week later, he received a letter from the hospital that said a test of his blood revealed that he could be a carrier for the hepatitis B virus (HBV). He was urged to consult his doctor.

David did not have any of the standard symptoms of acute hepatitis. His doctor ordered liver function tests for ALT, bilirubin, and other chemicals, which were normal; a coagulation test for blood clotting; and a blood test for the hepatitis B surface antigen (HBsAg), which was positive. The doctor agreed that David was probably a carrier of HBV. Since David had no symptoms and there is no treatment for the disease, the doctor advised him about precautions he should take to avoid transmission of the virus to others. He also interviewed David at length to determine how he may have been infected. Neither one of them could come up with a plausible scenario. David was scheduled to return to the doctor in six months for follow-up blood and liver function tests in order to determine whether he was a carrier with a chronic infection.

David was not one to sit around and wait for things to happen. He set about to learn all he could about his disease and tried to figure out how he fit into the picture. He also tried to find clues about how he could have been infected. He had to tell his family about his illness anyway, so he decided to ask them for ideas about the infection route. Valerie was upset by the news. As a nurse, she understood how HBV is transmitted. Neither she nor David's father and sisters had ever had symptoms or been diagnosed with hepatitis. She decided to have all of them tested for HBV. Of the five, only Valerie tested positive for the HBV immunoglobulins IgG anti-HBs and IgG anti-HBc, which are produced in response to HBsAg and the core antigen HBcAg, respectively. Both antibodies usually persist for a lifetime if the person recovers. Valerie realized that she must have had an acute, symptom-free HBV infection, possibly when she was pregnant, and may have given the virus to David. She could not recall how she was infected, but knew that as a nurse she could have been exposed to the virus many times. She also knew that chronic hepatitis B can ultimately cause cirrhosis or liver cancer. She was extremely upset and felt very guilty. David consoled his mother and reassured her that he did not blame her. It had just happened. He, too, was upset, of course, and continued to learn more about the disease.

Most children and at least half of all adults who are infected with HBV never experience the classic hepatitis symptoms. Neither Valerie nor David ever had symptoms. It is a mystery why symptoms do not occur, although it is known that the virus itself does not kill the host hepatocytes. Only the killer T cells do that, and they are the principal weapons of the immune response. It is possible that in many cases, the immune system gets the virus under control before enough damage is done to cause symptoms. About 90% of infected children and adults recover, as Valerie did. David was one of the unlucky 10%. However, about 80% of newborns develop chronic hepatitis, possibly because a newborn's immune system is not fully developed.

ABOUT HBV

The blood work from David's six-month follow-up visit was still positive for HBsAg. This result is considered diagnostic of a chronic HBV infection. The chronic phase develops when the immune system is unable to detect the virus in the hepatocytes. The virus can change its epitopes, for example, so that the B cells and killer T cells no longer recognize them as antigens. David is a carrier and will be contagious for many years. This fact severely limits his lifestyle because transmission of the virus involves exposure to infected blood or other body fluids. There are many precautions he has to take: He cannot donate blood. He should not participate in sports or other activities in which others could come into contact with his blood, sweat, tears, or saliva. Sports such as basketball, football, soccer, wrestling, and hockey should be avoided, although tennis, golf, and skiing are safe. He will have to clean his dishes and eating utensils very carefully to protect his family and friends. He will have to take great care to prevent exposing family members to his blood. For example, if he has open wounds or sores, or cuts himself while shaving and a drop of blood is left in the sink, a family member may come into contact with the virus. He should always use a condom when having sex and, thus, may not have children. He will have to see his doctor regularly so that both of them can follow the progress of the disease and watch for complications.

In the chronic phase of HBV, the virus continues to impair liver function and cause inflammation at modest levels. David could be symptom-free for 10 or more years. It is the cumulative effects of the killer T cells killing the hepatocytes over many years that ultimately cause serious liver damage. Time is the enemy in the chronic phase. Cirrhosis develops in about 30% of hepatitis B cases, and liver cancer develops in about 20% of cases after 10 years.

HBV

The hepatitis B virus is classified as an hepadnavirus. It is the only hepatitis virus that has DNA as its nucleic acid. Its nucleocapsid is spherical, as are those of all known hepatitis viruses, and it has an envelope. The envelope itself can have many shapes. The surface antigen HBsAg is in the envelope and its presence in blood is diagnostic of an active infection. This antigen is also known as Australia Antigen because it was first isolated in 1965 by Nobel Prize winner Baruch Blumberg in the serum of an Australian Aborigine. It was finally identified as being associated with hepatitis B virus in 1968 by virologist Alfred Prince.

Another antigen, HBcAg, is called a **core antigen** (part of the "core," or essential structure, of the virus) and can be very difficult to detect directly because it is shielded from the outside world by the envelope and the capsid. However, antibodies to HBcAg can be found in people with chronic infections or in those who have recovered from an acute infection. HBsAg can first show up in blood during the incubation phase a few weeks after the infection or may not appear until the completion of the prodromal phase a month or so later, but it is always the first antigen to appear in the blood. It persists in the blood during a chronic infection.

ROUTES OF HBV TRANSMISSION

HBV is a bloodborne virus that can leave the blood and enter other body fluids such as saliva, semen, tears, sweat, and vaginal fluids. HBV cannot survive in the intestines very well because the virus is attacked and destroyed by the bacteria that normally live there. Valerie had an acute infection from which she recovered, but we know that the infection could have been active during David's birth because of her handling of the bloody gauze and the scratch on her finger. David probably acquired his infection from Valerie's vaginal fluids at birth. This infection route is very common wherever the disease is **endemic** (common in a specific area). It is unlikely that David got the virus directly from his mother's blood because the virus does not cross the placenta and there is no other way he could have been exposed to Valerie's blood while in her womb.

HBV is considered more infectious than HIV, the virus that causes AIDS. Transmission from mother to child at birth is a common route. Needle sharing among drug abusers is another common route, especially in developed countries. Sex with an

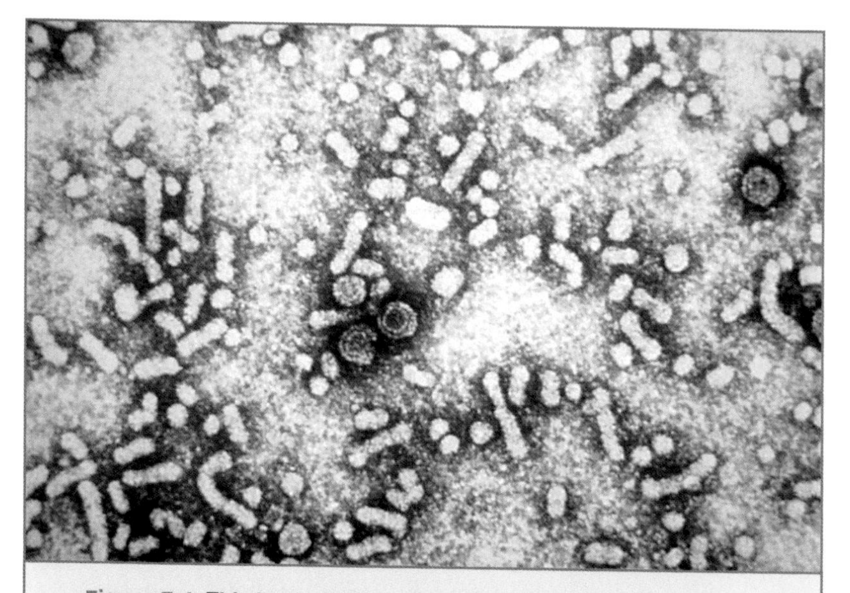

Figure 7.1 **This is an electron micrograph of hepatitis B virus particles. This is the virus that causes what is commonly called serum hepatitis. It is often spread by contaminated medical equipment and by the practice of sharing unsterilized hypodermic needles, as is often the case among IV drug users. (Centers for Disease Control and Prevention)**

infected person is dangerous. Accidental touching of infected body fluids and then touching the mouth, eyes, or broken skin is another route. Accidental needle punctures or scalpel cuts are serious occupational hazards for health-care workers. Another route is by deliberate puncture with improperly cleaned needles, such as in tattooing and acupuncture. Tools used in nail salons and barbershops can be contaminated, and this risk is especially high in areas where the virus is endemic. Finally, the sharing of toiletry articles such as toothbrushes, razors, razor blades, fingernail files, or nail clippers with family members can expose a person to the virus if the person has a cut or open sore that touches the contaminated tool or toiletry article.

TREATMENT

The acute phase of HBV is not treatable other than for symptom relief. Treatment for the chronic disease seeks to slow the progress of the disease and reduce infectivity. A really effective drug, one that can arrest or eliminate the virus completely, promote recovery, and last a normal lifetime, has not yet been found. The treatment of choice at this time is with a group of proteins called **interferons**. These are proteins that interfere with viral replication.

Two types of interferon are available to treat hepatitis B viral infections. Intron A (interferon alpha-2b) is used to treat chronic hepatitis B in patients one year of age and older. This is a recombinant form of interferon, meaning that it is produced by bacteria that have been genetically modified to make it. It provides several different activities to enhance the immune system, including induction of enzymes, enhancement of macrophage activity, and augmentation of the specific cytotoxicity of lymphocytes for target cells. Side effects include fever and flu-like symptoms, rapid heartbeat (tachycardia), low blood pressure (hypotension), irregular heartbeats (arrhythmias) in patients with underlying heart disease, possible depression and suicidal behavior, depression of bone marrow function leading to possible severe anemia, decrease or loss of vision, thyroid abnormalities, possible toxicity to the liver, and inflammation of the lungs and pneumonia. Nevertheless, the benefits do outweigh the risks.[1]

Another recombinant form of interferon is Pegasys (**pegylated** interferon). This form of the drug is used to treat adults only who are HBeAg positive and those who have HBeAg negative chronic hepatitis B who also have liver disease and enlargement. Its mode of action is similar to that of Intron A in that it also inhibits viral replication, and enhances the activity of the immune system. The side effects are also similar to those seen in patients using Intron A. These include neuropsychiatric reactions such as suicidal and homicidal behavior, depression, fever and flu-like symptoms, suppression of bone marrow leading to anemia, high blood pressure (hypertension), cardiac arrhythmias, chest pain and heart attacks, stroke, liver failure and an exacerbation of hepatitis, thyroid disease, diabetes mellitus, pneumonia and lung inflammation, colitis and pancreatitis, and possible loss of vision.[2]

A fairly new drug, called Epivir-HBV (lamivudine), that interferes with virus replication is also used. This medication is also used to treat HIV. It is not known to cause serious side effects and may be taken by both children and adults. The treatment with lamivudine consists of taking one tablet by mouth daily. This is a lot easier than receiving a regular series of painful injections of interferon for four months. However, the patient must take the drug for a lifetime because the drug only arrests viral replication; it does not kill the virus. A combination therapy with interferon-α and lamivudine has been studied for several years with mixed results. More studies are being conducted, and it is not available for routine use.

Hepsera (adefovir dipivoxil) is another oral drug that was approved in 2002 for treatment of chronic HBV in adults and children 12 and over in the United States. It can improve liver

INTERFERONS

Interferons are immune proteins that are produced by host cells in response to viral infections. There are three distinct types of interferons, called α (alpha), β (beta), and γ (gamma). They stimulate host cells to produce proteins that inhibit the replication of viral nucleic acid and the synthesis of viral proteins. Thus, they "interfere" with viral reproduction without killing the virus directly. Interferons also activate helper T cells and accelerate the activity of the B cells. Not all cells can produce interferons, and many cells can produce only one kind. White blood cells, for example, produce both α and β proteins. The interferon system does not always work well, and much research is devoted to understanding how it is regulated and how it may be activated by drugs. Other efforts are being made to use interferons as injectable drugs for a number of viral diseases, including hepatitis. Interferons α-2a and α-2b are approved in the United States for use in hepatitis B patients. These drugs do not always work, but they can be more effective than other drugs and may be the best that can be done at the present time.

function and reduce chronic liver inflammation and scarring by 50% to 65% in selected patients. The drug interferes with viral replication as does lamivudine, but it seems to work better. It has not been studied for use with interferon, and it can have serious side effects, including kidney damage, exacerbations of hepatitis, severe liver enlargement, and lactic acidosis. In addition, in 25% of patients, discontinuation of use can cause a viral rebound that makes the disease even worse than before treatment.

Another of the seven drugs presently approved in the United States to treat chronic hepatitis B is Baraclude (entecavir). This medicine is used in adults only who have chronic hepatitis B and persistent elevations of ALT and AST. It acts by interfering with

HBV DNA polymerase, which is an enzyme used by the virus to create DNA. Side effects include exacerbations of hepatitis when the drug is discontinued, lactic acidosis, and severe liver enlargement.[3]

A sixth approved drug is Tyzeka (telbivudine). This medication is used to treat chronic hepatitis B in adult patients with evidence of viral replication and either evidence of persistent elevations in serum aminotransferases (ALT or AST) or histologically active disease. It also acts by interfering with HBV DNA polymerase, which is an enzyme used by the virus to create DNA. Adverse reactions include fatigue, headache,

INCIDENCE, PREVALENCE, ENDEMIC, AND OUTBREAK

When health professionals talk about the occurrence of a disease in some part of the world, they try to use language that can be understood by all health professionals and to present information that allows comparison with occurrences elsewhere. *Incidence* refers to the number of new cases per year for a specified number of people, which could be 100, or 1,000, or 1 million people. It is not essential to know what the actual population size is when we express things this way. For example, the incidence of hepatitis B in the United States in 2002 was about 2.8 cases per 100,000 people per year, but that number may have been derived from a survey of the entire U.S. population. Prevalence is similar to incidence, except that the statistic includes all cases, new and old, per year. *Endemic* means that a disease has a fairly constant incidence over a long period of time. The level of incidence does not influence the decision to call a disease endemic in a geographical location as long as that incidence is above the average for areas with low incidence

cough, diarrhea, abdominal pain, dizziness, muscle pain, and insomnia.[4]

The last of the currently approved drugs used to treat chronic hepatitis B is Viread (tenofovir disoproxil fumarate). This medication is also used only in adults and has the same mode of action as the two drugs mentioned above. It is also used for HIV. Common adverse reactions are a rash, diarrhea, headache, pain, depression, asthenia (weakness), and nausea.[5]

David was eligible for interferon therapy and decided to try it despite the low success rate of the treatment and its side effects. Interferon can cause fever, fatigue, malaise, and

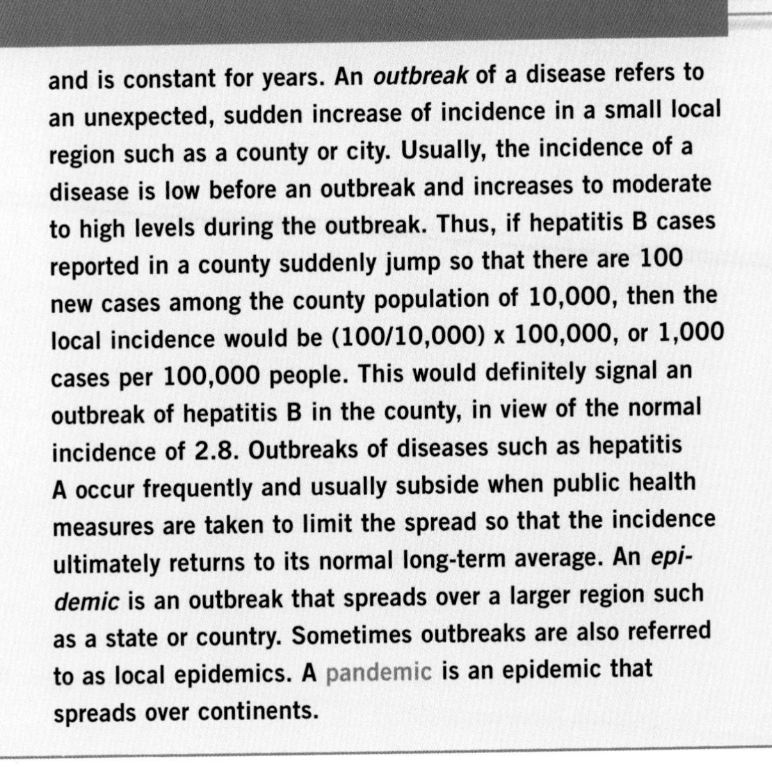

and is constant for years. An *outbreak* of a disease refers to an unexpected, sudden increase of incidence in a small local region such as a county or city. Usually, the incidence of a disease is low before an outbreak and increases to moderate to high levels during the outbreak. Thus, if hepatitis B cases reported in a county suddenly jump so that there are 100 new cases among the county population of 10,000, then the local incidence would be (100/10,000) x 100,000, or 1,000 cases per 100,000 people. This would definitely signal an outbreak of hepatitis B in the county, in view of the normal incidence of 2.8. Outbreaks of diseases such as hepatitis A occur frequently and usually subside when public health measures are taken to limit the spread so that the incidence ultimately returns to its normal long-term average. An *epidemic* is an outbreak that spreads over a larger region such as a state or country. Sometimes outbreaks are also referred to as local epidemics. A pandemic is an epidemic that spreads over continents.

suppression of white blood cells, but these effects disappear when the treatment is complete. He did suffer from fatigue and fever during the treatment, and he lost quite a bit of time from work because of it. However, upon completion of the treatment, he had no detectable viral DNA or viral antigens in his blood. The outlook for permanent remission was good and David was elated. He would have to be monitored at least yearly for the rest of his life to be on guard for a recurrence of virus activity.

WORLDWIDE OCCURRENCE AND PREVENTION

The World Health Organization estimates that about 2 billion people alive today have been infected with HBV. Nearly 350 million of these people are carriers. Additionally, about 600,000 people die annually due to the acute or chronic consequences of HBV. Hepatitis B is the most serious and important viral hepatitis in the world because there are so many carriers, it is so contagious, and its severe effects in the chronic phase cause terrible suffering and impose huge costs for medical care. Underdeveloped countries have the highest incidence because of lack of funds for vaccines and poor public health services. Hepatitis B is endemic in China and other parts of Asia. Most people in the region become infected with HBV during childhood. In these regions, 8% to 10% of the adult population is chronically infected. Liver cancer caused by HBV is among the first three causes of death from cancer in men, and a major cause of cancer in women. High rates of chronic infections are also found in the Amazon and the southern parts of eastern and central Europe. In the Middle East and Indian subcontinent, an estimated 2% to 5% of the general population is chronically infected. Less than 1% of the population in Western Europe and North America is chronically infected.[6] However, in the United States and other developed countries, less than 20% of the population has been infected and less than 2% are carriers (perhaps 1 million people). The lower incidence is due to a very effective vaccination program and screening of donated blood. Post-transfusion hepatitis B is rare in the United States. Neither Valerie nor David had been vaccinated, because until about 20 years ago, it was thought that the low incidence of the disease did not justify the cost of routine vaccination. Vaccination would not have helped David anyway, since he picked up the virus at birth.

A 95% effective vaccine for hepatitis B has been available for only about 30 years. The World Health Organization now recommends that all newborns be vaccinated for both hepatitis A and B, but this has not been feasible in many parts of the world because of the high cost and the difficulty of reaching people in remote areas. It has been standard practice in the United States and Europe to screen all pregnant women and vaccinate all newborns for hepatitis B only since 1991.

An unvaccinated adult should be vaccinated if he or she is at risk for exposure to HBV. Adults who may have frequent, direct contact with carriers, such as health care workers, drug users, police officers, and firefighters, as well as those who travel frequently to areas where HBV is endemic, should be vaccinated. An immunoglobulin specific for HBV is available but very expensive. It provides only short-term protection against infection and is recommended for newborns of mothers who are carriers, in addition to vaccination, and for adults who know they have been exposed to the virus within the past three days because it can work effectively to destroy the virus within that very narrow time frame. The World Health Organization has set a long-term goal of universal vaccination. It is working on financial, cultural, and political strategies to realize this goal.

8

Hepatitis D

Denise had always wanted to be a doctor. Even as a child, she felt that as a doctor she could help people everywhere, and this was extremely important to her. Once she earned her degree and her license, instead of opening a practice like most of her classmates, she joined Doctors Without Borders, an international organization of doctors who provide aid in almost 60 countries throughout the world. These countries generally tend to be underdeveloped, so sanitation and health care are limited.

Her first assignment was in Asia and, unfortunately, she contracted hepatitis B while working there to help bring health care to poor villagers. After a period of rest and treatment, she recovered and went back to work. This time, she was assigned to sub-Saharan Africa. She was excited about this new challenge and immediately went to work helping her charges.

Soon after her arrival, Denise began to feel very fatigued. She attributed this to her recent recovery from hepatitis B and felt that working slightly shorter days would help. After a few weeks of a reduced schedule, she was not feeling any less tired. In addition, she began running a fever, was nauseated, and suffered with bouts of vomiting. Soon she developed abdominal pain and noticed that her skin and eyes were becoming somewhat yellowed. Her first thought was that the hepatitis B had returned and that she had never really gotten rid of it.

Because Denise was serving in sub-Saharan Africa, her colleagues suggested blood work to rule out the possibility of hepatitis D, since it is most common in that part of the world. They drew a sample of her blood and had it tested for anti-HDV antibodies. The test came back positive, which was not surprising considering that, although the virus is not common in most parts of the world, it is quite common where Denise was working as well as *in the Middle East, northern parts of South America, and the Mediterranean region. Also, hepatitis D rarely occurs in healthy individuals, but it is able to replicate only in the presence of active hepatitis B infection (***coinfection***) or in an individual who has recently recovered from a hepatitis B infection (***superinfection***). The virus requires the presence of HBsAg to cause infection.*

Denise had to be very careful as patients with hepatitis D have the highest mortality rate (20%) of those suffering from any form of hepatitis. She had to stop working and begin therapy with interferon-α. This seemed to be the most effective treatment. If her liver began to become cirrhotic and fail, a liver transplant would become necessary.

A NEW HEPATITIS ANTIGEN

A new antigen was discovered in 1977 in the hepatocytes of a hepatitis B patient in Italy. The protein resembled the hepatitis B core antigen HBcAg in that it could be found only inside the host hepatocytes of patients with hepatitis B. However, the antigen was distinct from any known HBV antigen and was given the special name "delta antigen" because it was thought to be another HBV antigen. It was soon learned that patients with delta antigen produced antibodies to it. In 1980, the delta antigen was established as part of a new microbe, which was called the hepatitis delta virus. It is now more commonly called the hepatitis D virus (HDV), and the disease it causes is called hepatitis D. The unique feature of this virus is that it can cause hepatitis only with the assistance of HBV. HDV can cause very severe forms of acute and chronic hepatitis in patients with chronic hepatitis B.

HDV is rare in the United States and northern Europe, but common in countries surrounding the Mediterranean Sea and in Eastern Europe, Russia, some central African countries, and some Latin American countries (Figure 8.1). The lower incidence may be because the incidence of hepatitis B is much lower in the United States and Europe than elsewhere, thanks to effective vaccination and blood screening programs. Epidemics

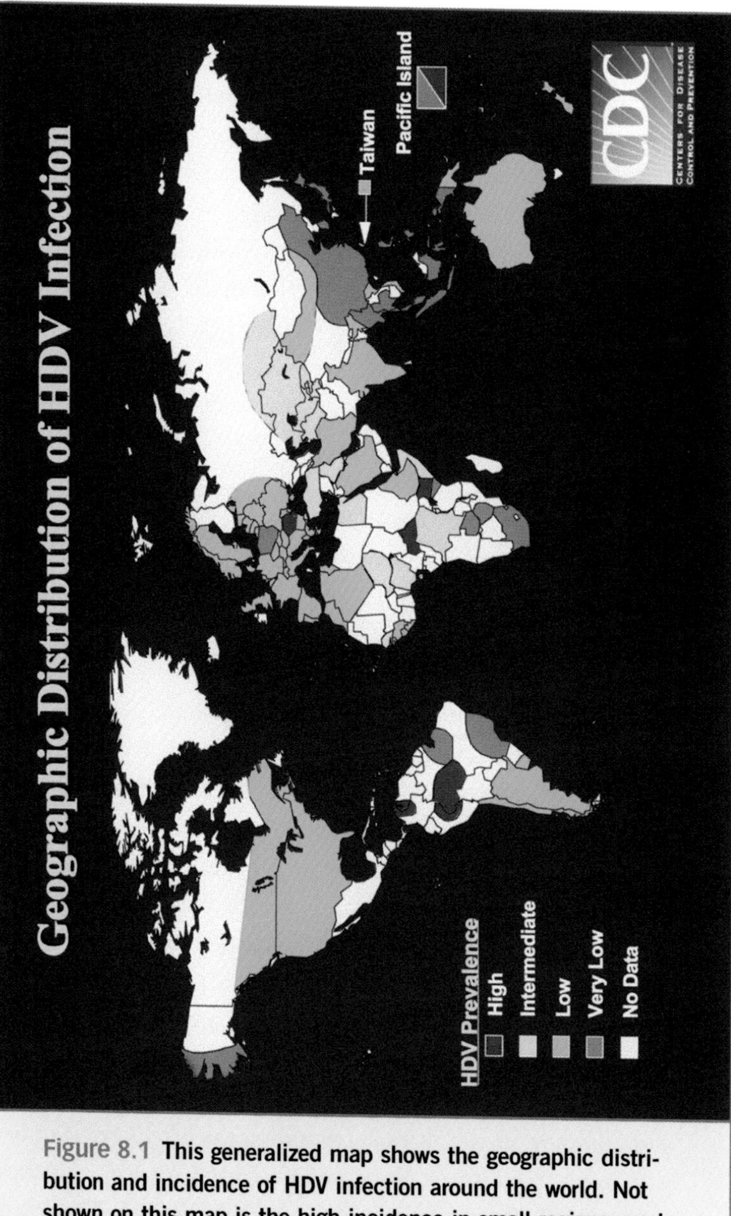

Figure 8.1 This generalized map shows the geographic distribution and incidence of HDV infection around the world. Not shown on this map is the high incidence in small regions, such as southern Italy or parts of Romania. There are also isolated regions of the Amazon River basin that have had many outbreaks of HDV among native tribes, with a high incidence of fulminant hepatitis. (Centers for Disease Control and Prevention)

have occurred among some native Venezuelan tribes, in areas surrounding the Amazon River, in Mediterranean countries, and in central Africa. HDV is endemic in Mediterranean countries. A high prevalence of HDV has been found recently in Albania, in some parts of China, in northern India, and in Okinawa. The World Health Organization estimates that more than 15 million people are infected with HDV worldwide. However, in countries that have adopted a stringent HBV control program, the prevalence of HDV is similar to that of HBV.

ABOUT HDV

HDV is unusual because it has single-stranded RNA that forms a closed circle and is the only known mammalian virus that does so. Its nucleocapsid has no well-defined structure, although it is probably spherical. The capsid has 60 copies of one protein, the delta antigen, HDAg. HDAg is the only protein encoded by the nucleic acid and is necessary for replication of the viral RNA and assembly of new virions. The nucleocapsid is enclosed by an envelope, but there are no spikes of HDAg on the surface. Thus, the immune system cannot easily recognize HDV as a new microbe. The envelope of HDV contains only the three forms of the HBV antigen HBsAg. This protein is essential for binding HDV to host cell receptors, for penetrating the host cell, and for assembling virions in the host. Some scientists consider HDV a subviral satellite of HBV.

HDV cannot reproduce without the help of HBV. It has no enzymes in the nucleocapsid and does not have genes for the enzymes that are needed for replication and protein synthesis in the host cell. HBV provides the necessary enzymes for replication and thus is a “helper virus” for HDV. When HDV is replicating in the host cell, HBV replication is turned off by HDAg. HDV commandeers all the HBV replication proteins.

TRANSMISSION OF HDV

To be infected by HDV, a person must also have HBV. HDV infection can occur in one of two ways. First, both viruses may infect at the same time. This is known as a coinfection. Second, a person with a chronic HBV infection can be exposed to HDV and become infected. This is known as a superinfection. HDV is a bloodborne virus like HBV and is transmitted in much the same way. The most common route of infection is by infected blood and blood products. Sharing of needles by intravenous drug abusers is a common route, especially in the United States and Europe. Unprotected sex, especially without a condom, is another common route of transmission worldwide. However, transmission from mother to newborn does not seem to occur.

VIROIDS AND SATELLITE VIRUSES

Viroids are infectious, virus-like microbes that have a single-stranded RNA that forms a closed circle; they have no capsid. The nucleic acid does not code for any proteins and must be replicated by the host cell. A helper virus for replication is not needed. Viroids infect plant cells and are a common problem in horticulture and agriculture. No viroids have been found in mammals, although some viruses that infect humans are similar to viroids. For example, hepatitis D virus is the only virus found in humans that has single-stranded circular RNA.

Satellite viruses, also called virusoids, have single-stranded RNA that forms a closed circle like that in viroids. Unlike viroids, the RNA encodes its own capsid protein. Satellite viruses replicate in the host cell cytoplasm using an RNA enzyme that is commonly found in plant cell cytoplasm but not in mammalian cell cytoplasm, and they require a helper virus to form their capsids. The RNA does code for some proteins. Similar viruses that infect animals, including humans, are also called satellite viruses because they must be closely associated with a helper virus. The hepatitis D virus is an excellent example of a satellite virus that infects humans.

COURSE OF THE DISEASE

The course of HDV depends on the way it is acquired. With coinfection (Figure 8.2), both acute hepatitis B and D develop. If the dose of HBV is large, symptoms develop and run their

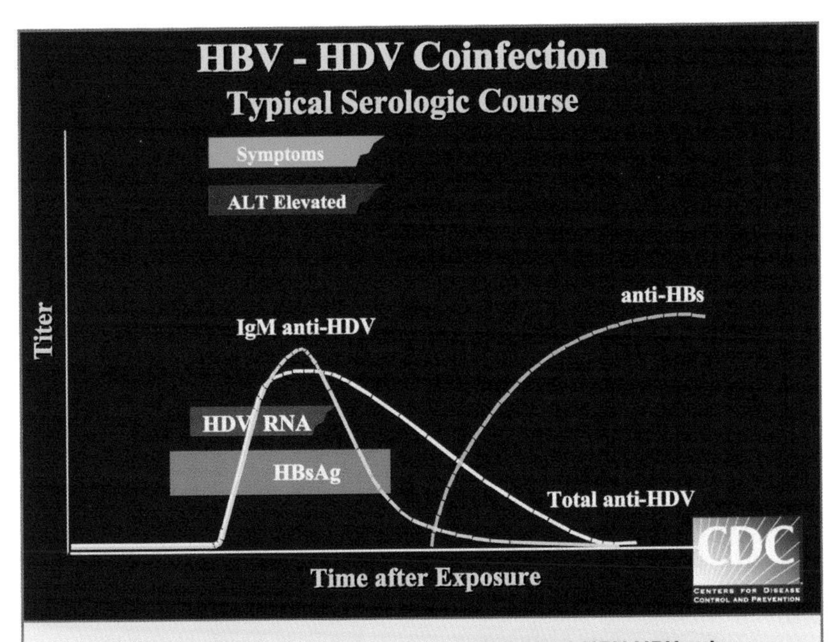

Figure 8.2 This graph shows how a self-limited HBV-HDV coinfection develops over time. "Titer" refers to the blood serum level of each substance. The horizontal bars indicate the time period over which the specified items can be observed or measured. Note that HBsAg and HDV RNA appear in the serum about the same time during the incubation period. This is the most communicable stage of the disease, since the person is unaware of the infection despite the very active virus in the blood. HBsAg (orange bar) disappears after a while, indicating that the person's immune system has successfully fought off the infection. The serum titer of anti-HBs (orange line) rises and remains high, which indicates a developed immunity for HBV. Since HDV and HBV are tied together, HDV-related substances rise initially and then disappear. That is what happens for the IgM anti-HDV (yellow line) and total anti-HDV (blue line) titers. Serum HDV RNA also disappears (magenta bar) when HBV declines, because HDV cannot reproduce. (Centers for Disease Control and Prevention)

course at about the same time. If the HBV dose is small, hepatitis B develops first and starts to resolve before hepatitis D expresses symptoms. In the latter case, the acute phase of the diseases lasts somewhat longer than if only an HBV infection had occurred. Coinfections are usually self-limited because the immune response to HBV effectively stops both viruses. Progression to chronic hepatitis D occurs in only 5% of cases.

Symptoms due to coinfection are likely to be more severe than for HBV alone. Disabling fatigue, lethargy, anorexia, and nausea develop first and last for three to seven days. Jaundice may then set in. Fatigue and nausea continue, urine turns dark yellow, and the stool becomes clay-colored. Symptoms subside as the immune system eliminates HBV, but fatigue may last longer than the other symptoms and prolong recovery time.

Superinfection is a far more serious process (Figure 8.3). Severe acute hepatitis D infection leads to chronic hepatitis D in 80% of cases. This happens because the immune system of a person with chronic hepatitis B has not been successful in eliminating the virus. In this case, HBV is always available to help HDV reproduce. During the early stage of superinfection, HBV replication is suppressed by HDV, and the D virus replicates. It is not understood why, but later, HDV replication subsides and HBV replication resumes. Symptoms during the chronic phase of hepatitis D are less severe than during the acute phase. Finally, late in the disease, either both viruses become inactive and remission occurs, or one or both of the viruses remain active. If both viruses remain active, then within 10 years, cirrhosis and liver cancer can develop as a result of chronic inflammation of the liver. These complications develop much more rapidly than with HBV alone. About 60% to 70% of patients with chronic hepatitis D develop cirrhosis and most die from liver failure. Fulminant hepatitis, though rare, is 10 times more likely to develop with a superinfection by HDV than with any other hepatitis virus infection. About 80% of patients with fulminant hepatitis die unless they can receive a liver transplant. About 20% of all patients with HDV die—a mortality rate about 10 times higher than that for HBV infection alone.

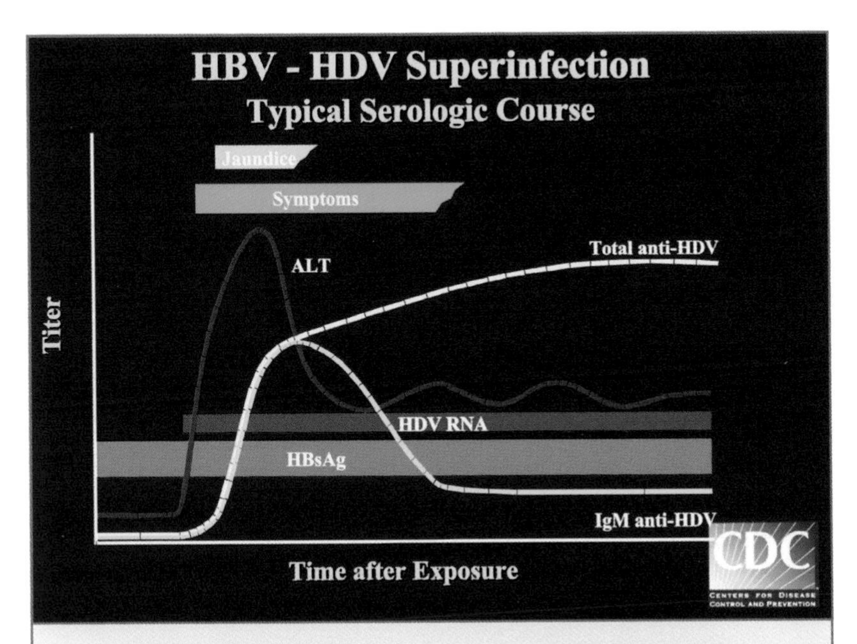

Figure 8.3 This diagram shows the course of HBV-HDV superinfection over time. "Titer" refers to the blood serum level of each substance. The time refers to the time after exposure to HDV. The person has already acquired a chronic HBV infection. Note that there is an incubation period for HDV. This is a typical record of a patient who has chronic hepatitis. The HBsAg titer (orange bar) is measurable but lower than for a pure HBV infection because HDV interferes with HBV reproduction. HDV RNA (magenta bar) appears and remains at measurable levels because the infection is chronic. Total anti-HDV (blue line) antibodies rise slowly and remain elevated due to the persistence of HDV. Note the high levels of serum ALT (red line) that indicate ongoing liver damage. Superinfections are far more serious than coinfections because they always result in chronic hepatitis with more severe symptoms that persist longer (green bar) and a very high risk of liver failure or liver cancer. (Centers for Disease Control and Prevention)

TREATMENT

No antiviral therapies are available for treatment of either acute or chronic hepatitis D. Interferon-α therapy, which targets the HBV, slows the progress of the disease and has caused remissions. But the therapy does not make the patient virus-free. An interferon-treated patient remains a carrier of HDV.

PREVENTION

The best way to prevent an HDV infection is to be vaccinated for HBV. People should take all the precautions recommended to avoid exposure to HBV. Anyone with chronic hepatitis B must be educated about the risks of acquiring HDV. Sharing of drug injection needles and unprotected sex are the two most important behaviors that should be avoided; the consequences of reckless behavior are severe.

9

Hepatitis C

Kevin was a 30-year-old African-American attorney working for a large law firm in Chicago. He became interested in his roots and started exploring his family history. He started with a family Bible that had been passed down from the time of the Civil War (1861–1865). He found that his great-great-great-grandfather was a slave on a plantation in Mississippi. So Kevin went to Jackson, Mississippi, and searched the public records stored down in a musty basement. He found that most slaves in that region came from West Africa in what is now the modern country of The Gambia. He could not find any information about his ancestor, but decided to visit The Gambia on his next vacation to pursue his roots further. Kevin learned to his delight that The Gambia is a terrific vacation destination. Situated on the Atlantic coast, it has a balmy climate year-round, miles of beautiful beaches, excellent hotels, very friendly English-speaking people, and few crowds of tourists.

Kevin was excited about his trip. He flew to Banjul, the capital city of The Gambia. But on the way to his hotel, the taxi he was riding in was involved in a terrible accident. Kevin was severely injured and was rushed to the hospital in Banjul. He needed emergency surgery and required a transfusion of one unit of blood. The surgery went well. Kevin's surgeon had trained at the University of Chicago Medical School, which took Kevin by surprise, so the two of them had lots to talk about.

Kevin spent the rest of his vacation in Banjul recuperating from the accident and the surgery. After flying home, he felt much better and was ready to return to work three weeks later. But all was not well. Three months after his return to work, Kevin began to feel unusually tired. He was an athletic person, but he could no longer finish a game of racquetball. He found it increasingly difficult to get through a typically busy day at the office. Kevin just thought he was in a slump after his trip and accident and that he would get over it soon enough. Then his wife noticed that the whites of his eyes were yellowed. She insisted that he go to see his doctor.

Kevin had only two of the symptoms of acute hepatitis—jaundice and fatigue—but his doctor suspected the disease when he heard about Kevin's trip to an underdeveloped country. Kevin could have been exposed to a hepatitis virus during the accident, during surgery, or from the blood transfusion. He also could have been exposed to one of the enteric viruses (viruses introduced through the intestine). Kevin had chosen to be immunized for hepatitides A and B before he went on his trip. A blood test was ordered for hepatitis C, and for hepatitides A and B, just in case the original vaccinations had not been effective. Results showed that Kevin had anti-HAV IgG, an antibody for HAV that is expected after recovery from an acute phase illness or after immunization. Of the three antibodies for HBV, the tests found anti-HBs and anti-HBc, but not anti-HBsAG. This pattern is expected after immunization. In addition, a second-generation enzyme immunoassay (EIA-2) was positive for hepatitis C antibodies. A follow-up recombinant immunoblot assay (RIBA-2) for HCV antigens was also positive and confirmed the EIA-2 results. These two tests became routinely available in the United States and other developed countries only in 1992.

The finding was that Kevin had acute hepatitis C. He was devastated and couldn't accept the diagnosis. He knew how serious the disease is and thought only intravenous drug abusers could get it. He sought a second opinion, just to be sure, and the diagnosis was confirmed. He realized he had to learn more about his illness. As he learned and understood more about how he became infected and how the disease can be managed, he gained hope that his future was not as grim as he thought at first.

ABOUT THE VIRUS

The hepatitis C virus (HCV) is classified as a flavivirus. It is a bloodborne, spherical virus with an icosahedral capsid and an

UNIT OF BLOOD

A unit of blood is a standard volume of blood that is recognized everywhere. A standard volume is necessary so that health workers all over the world know exactly how much blood they have available. One bag of blood, collected at a blood donor center or at a hospital, contains roughly one pint and comprises a standard unit of blood.

envelope. The nucleocapsid contains a single-stranded RNA. The virion is 40–60 nm in diameter. The viral RNA encodes a single, huge protein that is called a polyprotein because it is made up of several different proteins that are linked together end-to-end. After synthesis, the polyprotein is broken down by cell enzymes into 10 smaller structural and regulatory proteins. Core proteins and two envelope proteins are especially important products of this breakdown, as are several enzymes that are important for viral replication.

RNA-polymerase is a very important enzyme for replication of viral RNA, but the HCV enzyme has a defect. It is not able to detect errors during synthesis of new RNA like most other enymes of this kind. It may not notice, for example, if the code for the amino acid glycine is substituted by the code for the amino acid alanine in the replicating RNA. This defect actually works to the advantage of the HCV. There are two regions on the envelope protein E2 that have an extremely high mutation rate, thanks to this enzyme defect. Therefore, many mutants can be generated quickly, allowing HCV to evade attack by the immune system. Development of a vaccine for HCV has not been successful because vaccines are designed to mimic specific epitopes and thereby elicit an immune response with production of antibodies. It takes so long to develop and test a vaccine that by the time it is ready for use the virus has mutated and is unrecognizable to the antibodies induced by the vaccine. It is also thought that another enzyme encoded by the viral RNA specifically inhibits a critically important immune system molecule known as interferon-3 (INF-3). The loss of INF-3 activity effectively shuts down the immune response to HCV and allows the virus to replicate freely.

There are six major HCV **genotypes** (genetic makeup of an individual) with subtypes. Genotypes 1–3 have a worldwide distribution. Types 1a and 1b are the most common, accounting for about 60% of global infections. They predominate in Northern Europe and North America, and in Southern and Eastern Europe and Japan, respectively. Type 2 is less frequently represented than type 1. Type 3 is endemic in Southeast Asia and is variably distributed in different countries. Genotype 4 is principally found in the Middle East, Egypt, and central Africa. Type 5 is almost exclusively found in South Africa, and genotypes 6–11 are distributed in Asia.[1] Doctors seek to determine the virus genotype when they know a patient is infected with HCV because the duration and success of treatment depend on the type. Most Americans who are infected in the United States have type 1b, but Kevin had type 4 because he acquired it in Africa, where it is common. Type 1 infections require 12 months of treatment; all other types require only six months. Knowledge of the length of time needed for treatment is important because the entire treatment process is expensive and unpleasant.

HCV reproduction is very fast. A trillion (1 million-million) new virions can be made in a day, so that virus-free hepatocytes can be infected very quickly after the initial infection. Within days, at least half of all hepatocytes (liver cells) can be infected.

During the acute phase of HCV infection, the symptoms are mild. Only 10% of those infected have any symptoms at all. Kevin had two symptoms, and the fatigue was disabling. However, he was lucky, because his symptoms enabled early detection of the disease. He might have been a symptom-free carrier who discovered his illness years after liver damage was very advanced and he was showing signs of liver failure.

The immune system is not very successful in defeating the HCV virus. At least 80% of those infected develop the chronic disease. The primary immune response is cellular, involving killer T cells. The liver becomes chronically inflamed. Over a span of 10 to 20 years, scarring of the liver can develop into cirrhosis in 10% to 20% of infected people. Liver cancer develops in about 5% of victims after 30 years. The Centers for Disease Control and Prevention has summarized the progression of events associated with chronic hepatitis C infection. For every 100 people infected with the hepatitis C virus, 75 to 85 will develop chronic infection; 60 to 70 will develop chronic liver disease, 5 to 20 will develop cirrhosis, and 1 to 5 will die of cirrhosis or liver cancer.[2]

TRANSMISSION

HCV was originally called a non-A, non-B virus because it could not be isolated, yet it was known that a microbe caused a unique form of hepatitis. The virus was finally identified in 1989, and a reliable diagnostic test was developed in 1990. Routine screening of all donated blood became possible in developed countries in 1992. Before 1992, the most common route of transmission was by blood transfusion. Back then, the cause of hepatitis after blood transfusion was unknown, but it always developed after a blood transfusion and was called post-transfusion hepatitis (Figure 9.1). Routine screening of donated blood in advanced countries has eliminated this route of transmission. But because of the high cost and limited lab facilities for routine screening, blood transfusion is the main mode of transmission in underdeveloped countries. Gambia does not routinely screen blood for HCV even though its incidence is high in that part of Africa. Kevin unfortunately received a unit of blood that contained the virus and had not been screened.

HCV is transmitted almost exclusively by direct introduction of infected blood into the body (Figure 9.2), unlike

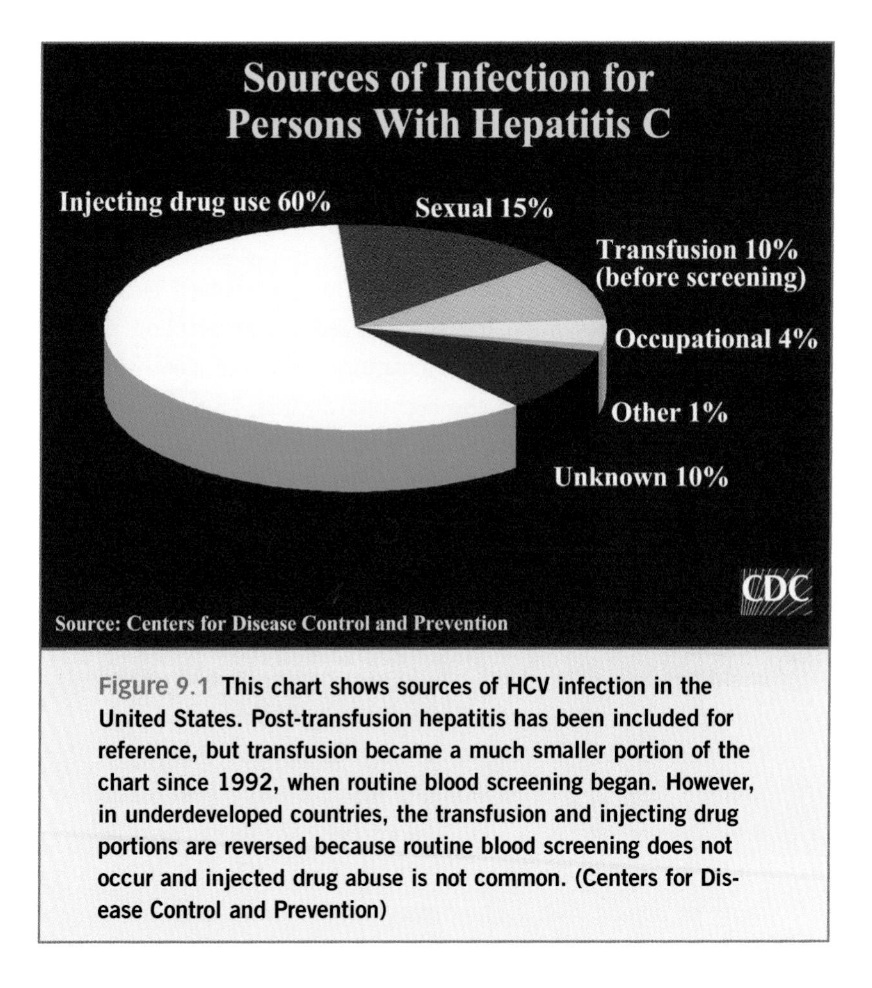

Figure 9.1 This chart shows sources of HCV infection in the United States. Post-transfusion hepatitis has been included for reference, but transfusion became a much smaller portion of the chart since 1992, when routine blood screening began. However, in underdeveloped countries, the transfusion and injecting drug portions are reversed because routine blood screening does not occur and injected drug abuse is not common. (Centers for Disease Control and Prevention)

transmission of HBV. In fact, HBV is far more infectious than HCV. Use of dirty needles by intravenous drug abusers is a very common cause of infection in the United States and other developed countries. Acupuncture and tattooing with improperly cleaned instruments and sharing a razor with an infected person can also introduce the virus, but are not significant routes of infection. You might expect that accidental needle punctures or scalpel cuts in health-care workers would be an important route of infection, but there is no evidence that these people have an above-average incidence of HCV overall.

TREATMENT

Current treatment for acute hepatitis C virus infection includes a combination of pegylated interferon-alpha-2a or pegylated interferon-alpha-2b and the antiviral drug ribavirin for a period of 24 or 48 weeks, depending on hepatitis C virus genotype. Sustained cure rates (sustained viral response) of 75% or better are seen in people with HCV genotypes 2 and 3 with 24 weeks of treatment. Sustained response is about 50% in patients with HCV genotype 1 given 48 weeks of treatment. In patients

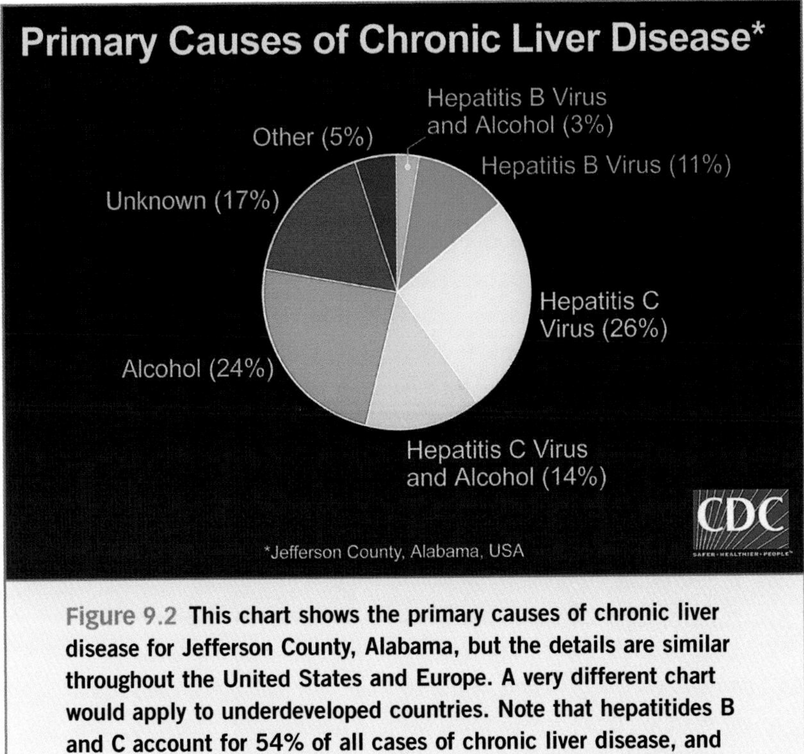

Figure 9.2 **This chart shows the primary causes of chronic liver disease for Jefferson County, Alabama, but the details are similar throughout the United States and Europe. A very different chart would apply to underdeveloped countries. Note that hepatitides B and C account for 54% of all cases of chronic liver disease, and that alcohol abuse alone accounts for 24% of cases. The recommendation that alcohol be avoided during a hepatitis infection is often ignored by patients. Alcohol abuse and chronic hepatitis account for 17% of chronic liver disease. (Centers for Disease Control and Prevention)**

PEG, INTERFERON, AND RIBAVIRIN REGIMEN

Interferon therapy for some genotypes of hepatitis C had been disappointing. Although positive effects were obtained, these effects did not last. The procedure required daily, or at best three times weekly, injections of the drug for up to one year. Side effects in some patients often required cessation of therapy. A new approach was developed. A molecule called polyethylene glycol (PEG) can be attached to an interferon α-2b protein to create PEG-IFN. This artificial pegylated interferon is more stable chemically in the blood, so only one injection per week is needed. Patients treated with this new drug have a much higher chance for a successful arrest of the virus than patients treated with IFN-α-2b alone.

Ribavirin is a drug that can be taken orally. It mimics the bases that are key parts of nucleic acid structure and interferes with proper reproduction of the viral RNA. It does not work for hepatitis C patients when given by itself, but when it is given in combination with PEG-IFN, it improves the success rate of the therapy. It also causes side effects in some patients, which may require cessation of therapy.

Combination therapy with PEG-IFN-α-2b and ribavirin is now the treatment of choice for chronic hepatitis C patients. It is also used for patients in the acute disease phase, with better results than those seen with chronic hepatitis C. In clinical trials, up to 20% of patients receiving combination therapy were unable to tolerate it. The treatment does not produce a cure, but removes the virus from the blood and retards or arrests the progression of the disease. An average success rate of 60% of those treated has been achieved, and scientists are working on ways to improve this rate.

with HCV genotype 1, if treatment with pegylated interferon and ribavirin does not produce a significant viral load reduction or complete clearance of RNA after 12 weeks, the chance

ANTIVIRAL SIDE EFFECTS

Interferon administration causes influenza-like symptoms in more than 60% of patients. Other side effects include chronic fatigue, depression, and mood disorders. Increasing the duration of therapy from 6 months to 12 months increases the likelihood of adverse effects. Treatment also may cause insomnia; rash and itching; anorexia; a large decrease in neutrophils (a type of white blood cell); a serious decrease in the number of blood platelets, which are essential for proper blood clotting; and abnormal function of the thyroid gland.

Treatment with ribavirin may cause hemolytic anemia. In this condition, there is a decrease in the number of red blood cells in the blood because the cells lyse, or "blow up." It can be a serious condition because red blood cells transport oxygen throughout the body and an insufficient number causes tissues to be oxygen-starved. Ribavirin can also cause birth defects and is not advised in pregnant women. Patients may develop a cough and have difficulty breathing. Rash and itching can also develop, as can insomnia and anorexia.

of treatment success is less than 1%. Sustained response is about 65% in those with genotype 4 given 48 weeks of treatment. Genotype 6 treated with the same medications for 48 weeks has a similar response rate as type 1.[3]

Specific antiviral drugs have been developed that show promise for treating the chronic disease, but they are extremely expensive. A combination of pegylated (man-made) interferon-α-2a or -2b (see sidebar, "PEG, Interferon, and Ribavirin Regimen") and ribavirin can be an effective antiviral treatment.

Treatment of chronic disease can eliminate the virus from the blood in up to 50% of those infected with the type 1 virus and in up to 80% of those infected with virus types 2 or 3. Elimination from the blood does not mean that the virus has been eliminated from all hepatocytes. It only means that virus replication has been slowed down and is less likely to cause serious liver malfunction or failure. Treated HCV carriers are also less infectious, although they definitely should not donate blood or organs. Such patients must be checked regularly for recurrence of an active infection. It may be necessary to repeat the treatment in the event of a recurrence. Serious side effects can be caused by the antiviral treatment, and patients must be monitored very closely.

Kevin decided to try the antiviral therapy despite the risk of serious side effects. He felt he had a good chance at arresting his disease because he was infected with the type 2 virus, which responds better to the treatment. His health insurance carrier agreed to cover the very high cost of treatment. Kevin's gamble paid off. His treatment was successful, his blood became virus-free, and he resumed a fairly normal life. However, he would have to be tested regularly for liver function, especially for blood levels of ALT and bilirubin, and for the presence of virus in his blood.

ALTERNATIVE THERAPIES TO TREAT HEPATITIS C

A number of alternative therapies have been used to treat hepatitis C in patients who did not respond to conventional medical treatment. There is no strong scientific evidence that these treatments improve hepatitis C. In cases where conventional treatment has failed to bring about the desired results, many patients have resorted to using one or more of these alternative approaches. These treatments are not a substitute for conventional therapy but may be an adjunct to it. Of course, the question arises as to whether or not it will bring about an improvement in the condition. The response in each case may well be different.

Ozone Therapy

Ozone is a form of oxygen that consists of three oxygen atoms in an unstable configuration. It exists naturally in the atmosphere, especially after a lightning storm where the high energy of the lightning causes the atoms to bond together. It also forms due to the action of ultraviolet radiation from the sun and exists in a layer above the earth that protects humans from dangerous ultraviolet rays.

Ozone is toxic to humans, but in extremely small concentrations, it has been used to treat a variety of diseases including hepatitis C. The main use of ozone is in a process known as ozone autohemotherapy (OAHT). When blood is exposed to a mixture of oxygen and ozone in the proper concentrations there is no apparent damage to the blood cells. Various protective mechanisms in the blood protect the cells from the oxidizing effects of ozone.[4]

OAHT is used in many countries in Europe, but not in the United States. Blood is collected in a glass container and treated with either heparin or sodium citrate so that it doesn't coagulate. It is then exposed to an oxygen/ozone mixture at a concentration of 15–80 μg/ml for five to 10 minutes and then returned to the patient's bloodstream. The procedure is repeated twice each week for seven to eight weeks. The treatment is used for a number of serious conditions including diabetic vascular disease, cardiac pathologies, viral infections of several kinds and, more specifically, hepatitis C, and a host of other diseases.

The rationale for using ozone is the observation that it causes the production of interferon alpha, beta, and gamma, interleukins (cytokines [chemical messengers] that help to stimulate the immune system by allowing communication between several of its component cells), the possible stimulation of other proteins, and an increase in the antioxidant defenses of the blood. The responses in patients have been observed to last for hours or days, suggesting that when white blood cells are activated by ozone, they migrate into lymph tissue and release the cytokines to stimulate other immune cells.

Milk Thistle

Herbals have been used for thousands of years to treat a myriad of conditions. Milk thistle (*Silybum marianum*) is one of these plants. Although considered a noxious weed, botanical practitioners in Europe have been using it for centuries to treat liver disease and jaundice and those in the United States also use it for liver disease.

It has been suggested that using the plant may help to protect the liver by promoting the growth of liver cells, inhibiting inflammation, and fighting oxidation (a chemical process known to damage cells throughout the body). A study supported by the National Institutes of Health, HALT-C (Hepatitis C Antiviral Long-Term Treatment Against Cirrhosis), showed that hepatitis C patients using milk thistle had fewer and milder symptoms of liver disease and an improved quality of life. However, there was no change in liver inflammation or virus activity. The researchers did point out, however, that the study was retrospective in that 23% of the participants were already using milk thistle at the time of enrollment into the study. They agreed that further, controlled research is necessary to make a definitive determination of milk thistle's medical properties.[5]

Ginseng

Asian ginseng (*Panax ginseng*) has been used for a number of conditions, including type 2 diabetes, erectile dysfunction, and as a stimulant. It has been tested in the laboratory on liver tissue and has shown some beneficial effects, but it has not been extensively tested in human subjects.[6]

Licorice Root

Studies performed outside of the United States have used glycyrrhizin, the extract of licorice root (*Glycyrrhiza glabra*), administered intravenously to treat hepatitis C. Initial findings suggest that there may be some beneficial effects on infected livers, but additional research in controlled studies must be performed before a true determination may be made of its efficacy.[7]

WORLDWIDE OCCURRENCE AND PREVENTION

The World Health Organization estimates that about 170 million people alive today are infected with HCV, with about 4 million of them in the United States. About 20% of all acute hepatitis cases are due to HCV, and about 10,000 deaths in the United States each year are the result of chronic hepatitis C. Medical care costs for hepatitis C in this country exceed $600 million each year. Most liver transplants in the United States are given to chronic hepatitis C patients. The number of new infections each year in the United States dropped dramatically from 240,000 in the 1980s to about 25,000 in 2001. Routine screening for HCV in donated blood is primarily responsible for this positive outcome. However, there is concern that increased drug abuse could lead to an increase in HCV in the United States. Worldwide, HCV incidence is increasing. The World Health Organization is working hard to reduce post-transfusion hepatitis C and is promoting education for intravenous drug users.

There is no vaccine for HCV. Prevention requires avoiding the common routes of transmission, which all involve direct introduction of the virus into the blood. Recreational use of intravenous drugs is never wise, but sharing of needles should be avoided. Sharing of other objects that could have infected blood on them, such as razors, toothbrushes, and the straws used to snort cocaine, can also lead to infection if the user has open cuts or sores. Tattooing and body piercing should be done only by someone who practices scrupulous hygiene and disinfection of their equipment.

10

Hepatitides E and G

Satya was 25 years old and living in Des Moines, Iowa. His parents had emigrated from Bangalore, India, to work at the University of Iowa in Iowa City, Iowa, where he was born and raised. Satya grew up hearing stories about family in Bangalore but had never been there. He knew his grandparents were aging, so he took a two-week vacation to visit them in Bangalore.

Satya enjoyed meeting his family, and his grandparents were thrilled. They had only seen pictures of him until now. He learned a lot about himself, his family, and India. He also loved the food! The fresh fruits and vegetables that could be purchased daily in the local open-air market were especially good, and he enjoyed the ritual of the trip to the market and bargaining with the vendors. Satya's visit was a great success and he left for home vowing to go back to India as soon as he could.

One month after his return to Des Moines, Satya became ill. First, he had flu-like symptoms—nausea, vomiting, and fatigue. Then a fever set in, his urine turned dark yellow, his stool became clay-colored, and his eyes yellowed. His doctor suspected hepatitis and did a series of blood tests for hepatitides A, B, and C to identify the specific disease. Satya had been vaccinated for hepatitides A and B as a young child. Test results showed that he had anti-HAV IgG, the antibody for HAV, and anti-HBs and anti-HBc, antibodies for HBV. There was no anti-HBsAg. Therefore, Satya was immune to hepatitides A and B, and could not have hepatitis D. An EIA-2 test result for hepatitis C antibodies was negative. Satya did not have hepatitis C but clearly had a form of hepatitis. When doctors do not know which virus is causing the disease, but can exclude some, as in Satya's case, they say that the patient has non-A, non-B, non-C, non-D hepatitis (or non-A, B, C, D hepatitis).

Tests for the remaining two hepatitides, E and G, are not routinely available because economical tests have not yet been developed. A friend of Satya's parents, a virologist at the University of Iowa Medical School, was doing research on hepatitis viruses. He was able to check Satya's blood for the immunoglobulins anti-HEV-IgMs and confirmed their presence. Satya had hepatitis E. Satya received the diagnosis about a month after he first became ill and was already recovering from the acute phase of the illness. His symptoms were less severe, and he was able to slowly resume his normal activities. The virologist told Satya that he should expect a complete recovery and then he would be immune to the disease for the rest of his life, since hepatitis E does not have a chronic phase. This is because the immune system can successfully fight this virus.

ABOUT HEV

The hepatitis E virus (Figure 10.1), HEV, was first identified in India in 1990. It was first classified as a calicivirus because of its structural similarities to other members of that family. This group causes diarrhea in children and adults and is a major cause of infant mortality in many parts of the world. However, further research has shown that it is really a member of the *Hepevirus* (not to be confused with the herpesvirus family) genus, but is not in any family at this time. HEV is spherical and the nucleocapsid encloses single-stranded RNA that can serve immediately as messenger RNA when released into the host cytoplasm. It has no envelope.

The immunoglobulins anti-HEV IgM and anti-HEV IgG appear in the blood by the time the icteric phase of the disease begins. These antibodies work effectively to destroy the virus over a period of a few months. The route of newly made enteric viruses is from the bile to the gut, from the gut to the blood, and then from the blood back into uninfected hepatocytes. The presence of strong antibodies in the blood thus catches all the new virions that would otherwise keep the disease going. Killer T cells

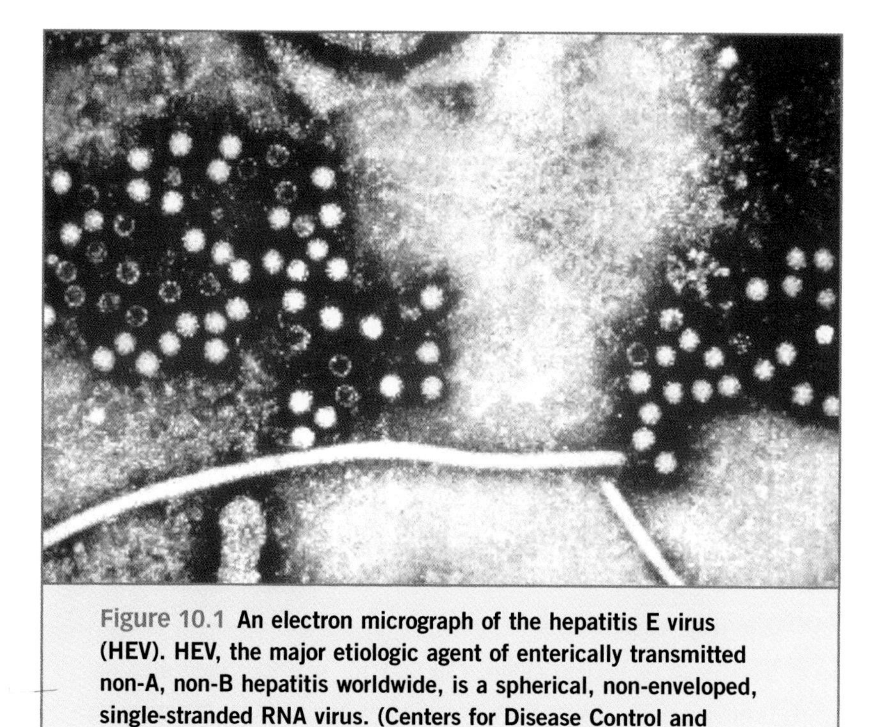

Figure 10.1 **An electron micrograph of the hepatitis E virus (HEV). HEV, the major etiologic agent of enterically transmitted non-A, non-B hepatitis worldwide, is a spherical, non-enveloped, single-stranded RNA virus. (Centers for Disease Control and Prevention)**

take care of the virus inside hepatocytes. Hepatitis E does not have a chronic phase, thanks to the strong humoral (body fluid) response. As a person recovers, anti-HEV IgM slowly disappears from the blood, but anti-HEV IgG remains to provide permanent immunity. The disease is fatal in 2% of those infected.

TRANSMISSION OF HEV

Fecal-contaminated water and food is the most common route of transmission. This is probably how Satya was infected. Either the fresh produce he ate so lustily in India was washed with contaminated water, or a vendor was a carrier who did not observe good personal hygiene. Uncooked or partially cooked contaminated shellfish is another route of transmission.

Transmission is strictly waterborne. Close person-to-person transmission is unknown.

TREATMENT OF HEV

The immune system does a good job of limiting HEV infection to an acute phase only. A victim can be very uncomfortable while experiencing symptoms and may be unable to engage in normal activities. However, recovery normally occurs within a few months of infection. Symptoms may be treated to decrease suffering, but there is no treatment for the disease itself.

WORLDWIDE OCCURRENCE AND PREVENTION OF HEV

In 1993, a team of researchers from the Walter Reed Army Institute of Research in Washington, D.C., began testing the efficacy of a vaccine for hepatitis E in Nepal. The vaccine could not be tested in the United States as hepatitis E is very rare here. However, in Nepal the disease is one of the leading causes of hospitalization during the flooding season.

In 2001, the king and his family were assassinated and there was a great deal of political turmoil and unrest. The research project almost collapsed because the testing of the vaccine was being done on soldiers and they were now involved in fighting a Maoist insurgency group. Nevertheless, the research team stayed to complete their work. In the end, the Walter Reed team and teams from GlaxoSmithKlein Biologicals were able to complete the research study.

The results were very encouraging. The vaccine proved to be highly effective as after three doses, only 3 of 898 soldiers who received the vaccine developed hepatitis E, whereas 66 of 896 soldiers who received placebos developed hepatitis E. This meant that the vaccine was 96% effective at preventing the disease. The trial also showed that when only two doses of vaccine

(continues on page 104)

TRANSMISSION OF VIRUSES BETWEEN DIFFERENT ANIMAL SPECIES

Most viruses have very specific host requirements. However, there are some important cases in which animal-to-human transmission of a virus can cause human disease. The transmission is not necessarily direct, although it can be. Rabies is a good example of direct transmission. A bite from a rabid animal can introduce the virus directly into a person's blood, and the virus can replicate in humans with devastating consequences. Influenza A virus has many forms, but all of them are carried with no ill effect by ducks. Occasionally, a new form of influenza A will be transmitted directly to humans, say by water contaminated by duck feces. Ducks can also directly infect other birds, such as chickens, producing avian flu. Chickens are often ground up for hog meal. Pigs that eat infected chicken meal can develop an influenza that can then be transmitted to humans either by direct contact or by contamination of water with their feces. There is one known case in which a human infected a pig and a flu epidemic among pigs followed.

The SARS virus has caused a great deal of concern worldwide because it causes a very severe infection and could cause a major epidemic or pandemic. SARS means "severe acute respiratory syndrome" and was first described in Asia in 2003. A global outbreak occurred after that, but it has been contained. The virus spreads through the air by close person-to-person contact, meaning that if an infected person is in proximity to a healthy person, the virus will be present in the air exhaled by the infected person and can be transmitted to a healthy person who inhales that air. It is believed that animals also carry the virus and can spread it to humans through the air or by direct contact with a carcass. Tens of thousands of animals were slaughtered in China after the SARS outbreak because of fear that they could be carriers of the virus. However, at this time, it is not clear whether animal-to-human transfer of the SARS virus is the main method of transmission. The human outbreak may have started this way, but control of the epidemic was achieved mainly by quarantine of infected humans.

Some viruses are transmitted by mosquitoes. The insect itself is not affected by the virus. It takes a blood meal from one animal that has a high virus count in its blood and then bites another animal. The second animal picks up the virus from the digestive fluids of the mosquito. The West Nile virus is a good example of this kind of transmission. Birds and horses are infected by this virus and can become sick and die. Mosquitoes bite birds, horses, and humans. Not only can a female mosquito transfer the virus from an infected bird to a human, but it can pass the virus on to her offspring in her eggs. Mosquito control is a major priority in all areas where West Nile virus has appeared.

The Ebola virus is extremely deadly. It has caused a major decline in the populations of great apes in Africa. It also infects humans and kills 90% of those infected. Humans can acquire the virus by direct contact with an infected ape or ape carcass. The hantavirus is another example. This virus infects rodents. It can cause serious respiratory inflammation in humans and is acquired by direct contact with the animals or by breathing dust contaminated with infected rodent dung. A serious outbreak of this disease occurred in the southwestern United States in 1993.

Certain species of African rats are popular as pets. These rats can be infected by the monkeypox virus, which is similar to the smallpox virus. Rats imported as pets in 2003 infected pet prairie dogs that then infected their owners. The infection causes a blister-like skin rash in humans.

Hepatitis E may also be transmitted from animals to humans. Domestic pigs are known to harbor the virus and transmission of the virus after consuming wild boar and undercooked deer has been reported.[1]

(continued from page 101)

were given, the success rate was 87%. In addition, the vaccine was safe and caused very few side effects.[2]

However, at this time there is no vaccine available for HEV. Clean public water supplies are the most important measure for protection of the public. Good personal hygiene, avoidance of uncooked produce and raw shellfish in areas where HEV is endemic, and drinking bottled water when traveling to areas with high incidence are prudent measures. Pregnant women are more susceptible than others to HEV, especially during their third trimester. Infected pregnant women have a 20% risk of developing fulminant hepatitis. They also have a high risk of premature delivery and a 33% chance that the baby will die. Pregnant women should avoid travel to areas with high incidence of HEV (Figure 10.2).

HEV is very rare in the United States, Canada, and Western Europe. However, there is some concern that HEV in pigs could infect humans, and this possibility is being watched closely.

Outbreaks of HEV are common in tropical and subtropical areas where there is poor sanitation but are rare in temperate areas. Outbreaks tend to occur during the monsoon season after heavy flooding that contaminates wells or when raw sewage gets into a city water treatment plant.

HEV is endemic (Figure 10.2) in Algeria, Bangladesh, Borneo, China, Egypt, Ethiopia, Greece, India, Indonesia, Iran, Ivory Coast, Jordan, Libya, Mexico, Myanmar, Nepal, Nigeria, Pakistan, southern Russia, Somalia, eastern Sudan, and the Gambia. In Egypt, about 60% of adults are positive for anti-HEV IgG. It is thought that children are infected with HEV early in their lives and have no symptoms, like with HAV.

G. B.

G. B. was a young surgeon who contracted a mild case of acute hepatitis in the 1970s. It is not known how G. B. was infected,

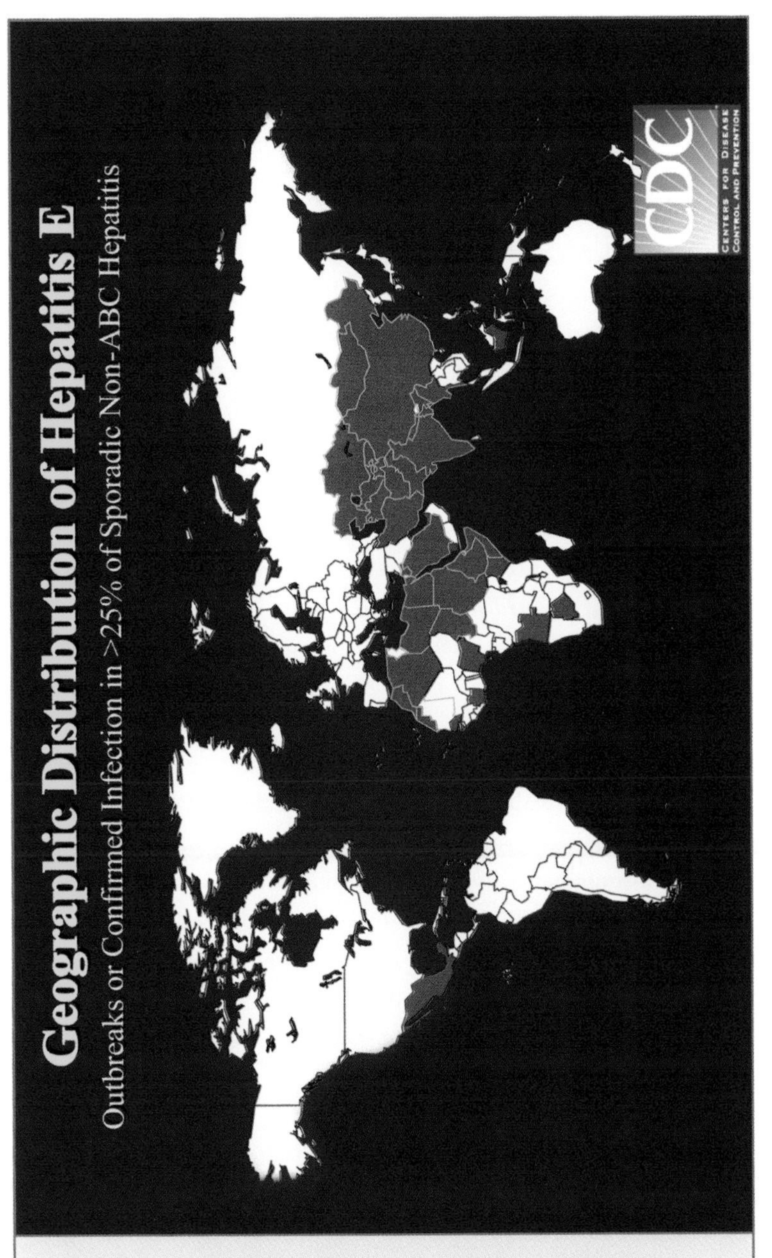

Figure 10.2 **This chart shows the worldwide occurrence of hepatitis E. Note that HEV occurs mainly in underdeveloped countries that have poor environmental sanitation. (Centers for Disease Control and Prevention)**

but it may have occurred when he cut himself with a scalpel during surgery. Tests for hepatitides A and B were negative. This occurred before the identification of HCV, so he was considered to have non-A, non-B hepatitis. His serum was used to inoculate monkeys to identify the virus. This was a standard approach to find new viruses at that time, but the efforts met with no success. Efforts to isolate G. B.'s virus continued for about 20 years until 1995. Then, thanks to more modern techniques, researchers were able to isolate three different viruses from monkey serum. These were named GBV-A, GBV-B, and GBV-C after the surgeon, G. B. It was determined that the first two viruses were specific to the tamarin monkey from which they were isolated, but that GBV-C could be the virus that had caused G. B.'s hepatitis. There had been many reports of non-A, non-E hepatitis, many of which were probably transfusion infections. About the same time, other researchers had isolated a new virus from a human with non-A, non-E hepatitis. They called the new virus hepatitis G virus (HGV). A year later, it was shown that GBV-C and HGV were the same virus.

The symptoms of hepatitis G are very mild versions of the standard acute hepatitis symptoms. Some scientists think that the virus is persistent but does not cause the liver complications of other chronic hepatitis virus infections. HGV is often found together with HCV, but there is no evidence that HGV aggravates the illness the way HDV aggravates an HBV infection. HGV is a bloodborne virus and is transmitted in the same way as HCV. Most experts now believe that HGV is not responsible for any serious acute or chronic hepatitis.

ABOUT HGV

HGV is a flavivirus like HCV, but its genome has little in common with that of HCV. HGV is a genetically distinct virus that contains a single-stranded RNA. It is spherical, and has an envelope. The replication process is probably similar to that of HCV. Structural and nonstructural proteins have been identified, but at present no reliable blood test for HGV antigens or anti-HGV proteins has been developed. Positive identification of HGV requires research laboratory–level testing that is too difficult and expensive for routine use. Little else is known about the virus.

TRANSMISSION OF HGV

Exposure to contaminated blood is the most common route of HGV infection. Post-transfusion hepatitis that still occurs in developed countries that routinely screen donated blood for the hepatitis A–C viruses is thought to be caused by HGV. Newborns can acquire the virus from their mothers, but babies seem to tolerate the virus well and develop immunity without showing symptoms. It is also possible that HGV is transmitted sexually, but there is limited information about this route at this time.

WORLDWIDE OCCURRENCE AND PREVENTION OF HGV

HGV has been found worldwide, but does not cause epidemics. There is no vaccine for HGV. The same precautions that are used to avoid HCV should be used for HGV. An estimated 30% of people in some regions are infected with HGV, including many drug abusers who are also infected with HCV. One U.S. study found that 18% of non-A, non-B hepatitis patients had HGV, and 80% of those patients also had HCV. Another U.S. study found that about 15% of chronic hepatitis C patients also are infected with HGV.

The story of HGV is still being written. This virus is found co-infecting people with hepatitis C who also suffer with cirrhosis or liver carcinoma, but its role in these illnesses is unclear. The effects of a pure HGV infection have been difficult to study because it is so closely associated with HCV. Although experts now believe HGV is not an important cause of acute or chronic hepatitis or a serious threat to public health, further study of the virus and its effects on humans may eventually change that view. One very practical reason for continuing research on this virus is the question of whether or not to screen donated blood for HGV. If HGV causes no serious or long-term effects, then it would be a tragic waste of donated blood if screening were implemented and infected blood discarded. Similarly, it could be a tragic error to assume that the question is settled and stop research on the medical consequences of HGV infection.

11

Conclusion

Mike's doctor had ordered serological tests to check for hepatitides A, B, and C. He knew Mike had been vaccinated, but sometimes the vaccinations don't work. Immunity to HAV is thought to last a lifetime, but HBV immunity can wane after 10 years or more in some people. The results showed that Mike was still immune to HAV and HBV. The EIA-2 test for anti-HCV antibodies was positive, and this finding was confirmed with an RIBA-2 test. A six-month follow-up showed that Mike was still HCV-positive. The likelihood was that he would develop chronic hepatitis C. Liver function tests were then done, and Mike's serum ALT level was high. This measurement provided an important baseline for monitoring the progress of Mike's disease.

The liver specialist to whom Mike was referred wanted to see him every six months to check on the progress of the infection. Serological tests and liver enzyme measurements were done. On Mike's first visit, the specialist also checked the virus genotype because this information can influence the treatment. Mike had HCV type 1b—common among drug abusers in the United States. Unfortunately, it is the most difficult type to treat.

Mike talked to the specialist about how he could have acquired the virus. This time, he was honest about his one-time experiment with cocaine. The doctor explained that it was possible to acquire the virus this way, although it is not a common route. Dirty needles used by intravenous drug abusers are the most common source of infection in the United States. In Mike's case, he inserted a snorting straw into his nose, where it may have either scraped the soft tissue in his nose and caused some minor bleeding or simply rubbed against an open sore. This blood contact must have happened at least twice in Mike's case. First, it happened to the carrier, who might not have noticed such a minor injury. Then, it happened to Mike, who also didn't notice his own injury. The doctor suggested that Mike talk to the three other people who shared the straw that night and urge them to be checked for HCV.

Mike was too young to be a candidate for the PEG-INF plus ribavirin treatment (see Chapter 9) because children and young adults under age 19 can develop serious side effects. His symptoms had disappeared and he was living a normal life, except that he had to see the liver specialist every six months for testing. Three years later, Mike's serum ALT levels were showing a pattern of consistent increase and his serum albumin level was decreasing. This is a red flag for serious liver damage, but it does not prove that the disease is progressing. As a precaution, the specialist ordered a liver biopsy. This procedure is not routine because it is expensive and unpleasant to undergo. However, it is the one reliable way of judging the extent of liver damage and the likelihood of future liver damage. The biopsy showed that Mike's disease had caused significant liver damage (Figure 11.1) and that the disease would likely progress to cirrhosis.

By this time, Mike was old enough to be eligible for PEG-INF plus ribavirin therapy. His liver was still intact enough that it could continue to function well if HCV replication was arrested. He was young and otherwise healthy, and the disease was threatening to get worse. If the disease was left unchecked, Mike would be likely to develop cirrhosis and ultimately need a liver transplant (if he could get one). The odds of success for this therapy were only fair, given that Mike was infected with the type 1b virus. However, the benefits far outweighed the risks in Mike's mind. He agreed to try it.

Mike's course of treatment was planned to continue for one year, with weekly injections of PEG-INF and a daily oral dose of

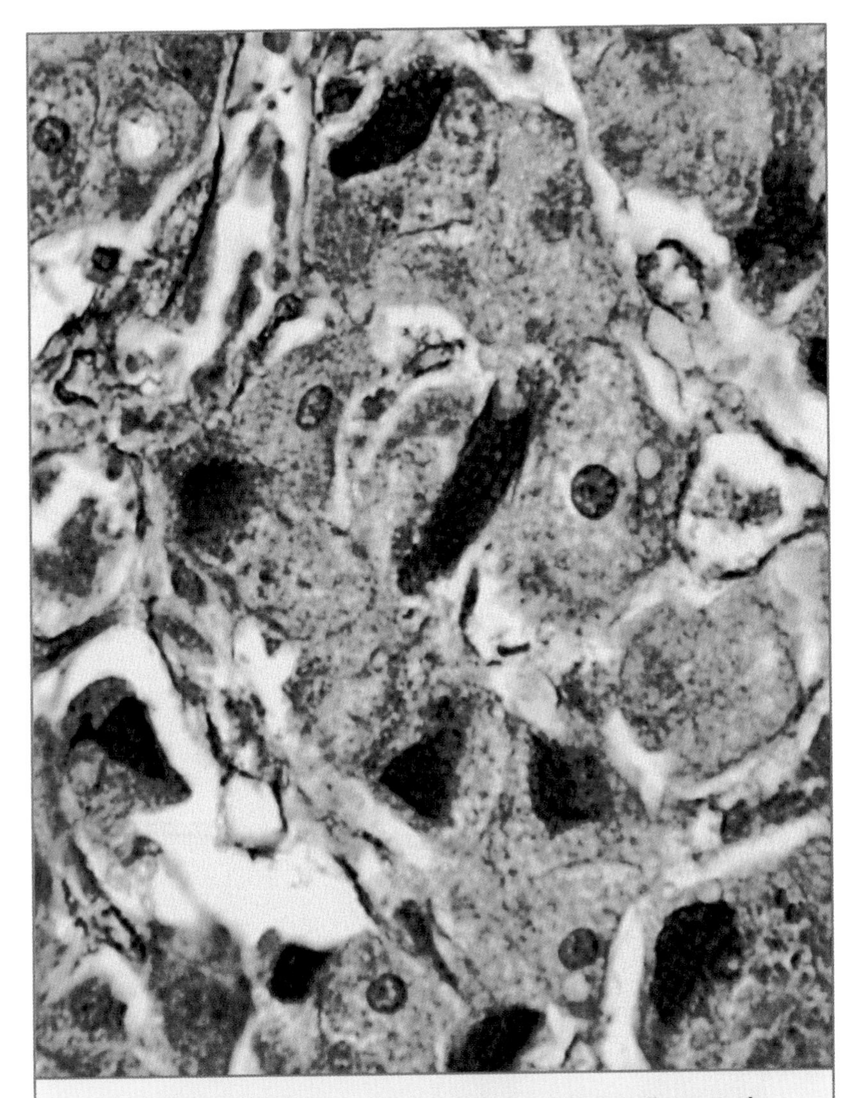

Figure 11.1 This light microscope image of a human liver sample infected with hepatitis (magnified 200 times) has numerous darkly stained irregular structures that are called plaques. Plaques are formed when infected hepatocytes are destroyed by killer T cells. Accumulation of plaques leads to cirrhosis and ultimately to liver failure. A large number of plaques seen in a liver biopsy would suggest that serious liver failure is likely to occur in the future. (Centers for Disease Control and Prevention)

ribavirin. His initial response was typical: fatigue, nausea, rash, and irritability on occasion. All this would have been bearable, but 4 months after the start of therapy, Mike's blood work provided some ominous information. He was developing hemolytic anemia, a decrease in the number of red blood cells caused by the cells lysing, or "blowing up." It can be a serious condition because the red blood cells transport oxygen throughout the body and having too few of them causes tissues to be oxygen-starved. Mike noticed that he was bleeding from his gums after brushing his teeth. Mike's blood platelet level was dropping to dangerously low levels. Platelets are an essential part of the blood-clotting process, and a lack of platelets places a person at high risk for bleeding to death. The treatment was stopped.

Mike's options for dealing with his disease were now much more limited. He could try another treatment course in a year or so, but in the meantime, liver damage would be progressing; he could do nothing and take the chance that he would not develop cirrhosis; or, he could be placed on the waiting list for a liver transplant. The decision was made to place Mike on the transplant waiting list, but only if another treatment course, which was adjusted to deal with the complications he had suffered, failed. Mike is still awaiting the outcome.

SUMMARY

Viral hepatitis proceeds through two stages. All forms have an acute stage, but only hepatitides B, C, and D have the second, or chronic, stage. The acute stage has four phases, not all of which are always observable. The incubation phase starts with the entry of virus into the body and is always symptom-free. However, the virus replicates actively at this time, is present in the blood, and, for enteric viruses, is shed in the feces. Carriers are most infectious during this incubation phase of acute hepatitis when they don't even know they are infected. The prodromal phase begins with the onset of symptoms, if any occur; otherwise, it begins when antibodies to the viral antigens first appear in the blood. Three to 10 days later, the icteric phase begins and lasts about four weeks. Jaundice may develop, but in most patients it does not. Serum antibodies climb to some of their highest levels during this phase. Finally, the recovery phase sets in if the immune system is able to defeat the virus. Recovery lasts four to eight weeks. Symptoms fade away slowly and the patient returns to normal. Serum antibodies for the virus remain to provide permanent immunity against reinfection.

Chronic hepatitis begins when there is evidence of active infection for six or more months. The chronic stage has three phases, but these do not occur in a one-time sequence. The phases can recur repeatedly. The replicative phase can last up to three years. The virus replicates actively, with significant viremia. The disease is most contagious during this phase. The seroconversion phase is the period during which the immune system produces antibodies and aggressively attacks infected cells. A change in the antibodies is seen in the blood, and serum ALT levels can be high because of the destruction of up to 10% of liver cells per year. Finally, the nonreplicative phase sets in, during which the virus is inactive and almost disappears from the blood; it is lying in wait within host cells. However, a new replicative phase can arise at any time to initiate a new cycle or not at all.

All forms of hepatitis have symptoms in common, most of which are experienced primarily in the acute stage of the disease. It is significant that many people never experience symptoms or do so late in the course of a chronic infection. This means that the disease can proceed to destroy the liver without the victim knowing it until it is too late. It also means that spread of hepatitis by carriers is a serious public health problem.

The most common symptoms are flu-like—nausea, vomiting, abdominal pain, fever, muscle aches and pains, and fatigue. Anorexia can also develop, followed by jaundice and itching.

Fatigue may persist for months. Itching always develops in the recovery phase of the acute stage, if at all. Symptoms usually recede by the end of the acute stage, but they may recur during the chronic stage. Fatigue is probably the most common chronic-stage symptom and may or may not be disabling.

Appendix

Table 1.1 Key Facts About Hepatitis Viruses

Virus	Class	Transmission	Nucleic Acid	Envelope	Chronic Phase	Incubation Time (weeks)
A	Waterborne	Fecal/oral	RNA	No	No	2–7
B	Bloodborne	Parenteral and Sexual	DNA	Yes	Yes	6–23
C	Bloodborne	Parenteral	RNA	Yes	Yes	2–25
D	Bloodborne	Parenteral	RNA, partial circle	Yes, comes from HBV	Yes, requires chronic HBV	2–8
E	Waterborne	Fecal/oral	RNA	No	No	2–9
G	Bloodborne	Parenteral	RNA	Yes	Yes	Unknown

Terms:

- **Waterborne** refers to enteric viruses (viruses that enter the blood from the gut) that are transmitted primarily by drinking contaminated water.
- **Bloodborne** refers to viruses that are transmitted by direct entry into the blood and can survive only in blood.
- **Fecal/oral** transmission means that the virus is shed in the feces and is often acquired by way of the mouth by drinking contaminated water or placing contaminated objects in the mouth.
- **Parenteral** transmission means that the virus can enter the blood by all possible routes except the gut.

Table 1.2 Viral Transmission Routes

Route	HAV	HBV	HCV	HDV	HEV	HGV
Contaminated food	Yes	No	No	No	Yes	No
Contaminated drinking water	Yes	No	No	No	Yes	No
Raw shellfish	Yes	No	No	No	Yes	No
Within family	Yes	Yes	Possible	Yes	Yes	No
Injectable drug abuse	Possible	Yes	Yes	Yes	?	?
Blood transfusion	Rare	Yes	Yes	Yes	Rare	?
Sexual contact	Yes	Yes	Rare	Yes	?	?
Oral contact	No	Yes	Rare	?	No	?
Mother/baby	No	Yes	Rare	No	?	?

Terms:

- "?" means that not enough is known about the topic.
- **Possible** means that transmission can occur theoretically, but that the route has not been established.
- **Rare** means that the route has been established, but it is unusual.
- **Within family** refers to any possible ways that family members come into contact, such as sharing eating utensils, razors, toothbrushes, or food handling.
- **Sexual contact** refers to sexual intercourse, including anal intercourse.
- **Oral contact** refers to kissing or oral/anal sex.
- **Mother/baby** refers to transmission to the newborn from the mother's vaginal fluids during birth.

Table 1.3 Diagnostic Serology*

Type	Stage	Serum Antigens and Antibodies
Hepatitis A	Acute phase only	Anti-HAV-IgM, anti-HAV-IgG
Hepatitis B	Acute phase	HBsAg, anti-HBc-IgM, anti-HBs-IgG, anti-HBc-IgG
	Chronic phase	HBsAg, HBeAg, anti-HBc-IgG, HBV-DNA
Hepatitis C	Acute and chronic phases	Anti-HCc-IgG, plus other anti-HCV antibodies
Hepatitis D	Acute coinfection	HBsAg, anti-HBc-IgG, anti-HD-IgM, HDAg, HbsAg
	Acute superinfection	Anti-Hbe-IgM, anti-HD-IgM, HBsAg, anti-HBe-IgM
	Chronic	Other anti-HDV antibodies
Hepatitis E	Acute	Anti-HEV-IgM early, anti-HEV-IgG late
Hepatitis G	All stages	HGV-RNA

* The table summarizes the serum antigens (Ag) and antibodies (Ig or the prefix anti-) that can be found by serological tests for each form of hepatitis. Bear in mind that these substances appear and disappear, depending on the stage of the disease as well as the phase of each stage, and are never all present at the same time.

Notes

Chapter 2

1. Geri R. Brown and Kim Persley, "Hepatitis A Epidemic in the Elderly," *Southern Medical Journal* 95, 8 (August 2002): 826–833.
2. Maurizio Bonacini, "Reactivation of Hepatitis B," *Liver Newsletter*, Liver Transplant Program and Center for Liver Disease, University of Southern California Department of Surgery, http://www.surgery.usc.edu/divisions/hep/livernewsletter-reactivationofhepatitisb.html (accessed on January 13, 2011).
3. Ibid.
4. M. G. Rumi, et al., "Hepatitis C Reactivation in Patients with Chronic Infection with Genotypes 1b and 2c: a Retrospective Cohort Study of 206 Untreated Patients," *Gut, An International Journal of Gastroenterology and Hepatology* 54, 3 (March 2005): 402–406, http://gut.bmj.com/content/54/3/402.abstract (accessed January 13, 2011).
5. National Digestive Diseases Information Clearinghouse, "Chronic Hepatitis C: Current Disease Management," January 2010, http://digestive.niddk.nih.gov/ddiseases/pubs/chronichepc/ (accessed on January 13, 2011).

Chapter 3

1. Katie Scarlett Brandt, "A Medical First, 20 Years Later," Comer Children's Hospital, The University of Chicago, September 2009, http://www.uchicagokidshospital.org/specialties/transplant/patient-stories/alyssa-liver.html (accessed January 16, 2011).

Chapter 7

1. U.S. Food and Drug Administration–Product Information, "Intron A," http://www.accessdata.fda.gov/drugsatfda_docs/label/2007/103132s5096lbl.pdf (accessed January 21, 2011).
2. U.S. Food and Drug Administration–Product Information, "Pegasys," http://www.accessdata.fda.gov/drugsatfda_docs/label/2009/103964s5147,%20103964s5163lbl.pdf (accessed January 21, 2011).
3. U.S. Food and Drug Administration–Product Information, "Baraclude," http://www.accessdata.fda.gov/drugsatfda_docs/label/2010/021797s011lbl.pdf (accessed January 21, 2011).
4. U.S. Food and Drug Administration-Product Information, "Tyzeka," http://www.accessdata.fda.gov/drugsatfda_docs/label/2010/022011s006,022154s003lbl.pdf (accessed January 21, 2011).
5. U.S. Food and Drug Administration-Product Information, "Viread," http://www.accessdata.fda.gov/drugsatfda_docs/label/2010/021356s035lbl.pdf (accessed January 21, 2011).
6. World Health Organization, "Hepatitis B," August 2008, http://www.who.int/mediacentre/factsheets/fs204/en/ (accessed January 22, 2011).

Chapter 9

1. World Health Organization, Global Alert and Response, "Hepatitis C," http://www.who.int/csr/disease/hepatitis/whocdscsrlyo2003/en/index2.html#HCV (accessed January 23, 2011).
2. Centers for Disease Control and Prevention, "Hepatitis C: General Information," http://www.cdc.gov/hepatitis/hcv/pdfs/hepcgeneralfactsheet.pdf (accessed February 18, 2011).
3. M. L. Shiffman et al., "Peginterferon Alfa-2a and Ribavirin for 16 or 24 weeks in HCV Genotype 2 or 3," *New England Journal of Medicine* 357, 2 (July 2007): 124–34; James Fung et al., "Chronic Hepatitis C Virus Genotype 6 Infection: Response to Pegylated Interferon and Ribavirin," *Journal of Infectious Diseases* 198, 6 (September 15, 2008): 808–812, http://jid.oxfordjournals.org/content/198/6/808.full.pdf+html (accessed January 23, 2011).
4. N. Di Paolo, V. Bocci, and E. Gaggiotti, "Ozone Therapy," *International Journal of Artificial Organs* 27, 3 (2004): 168–175, http://www.ossigenoozono.it/Ozone%20therapy.htm (accessed January 24, 2011).
5. National Center for Complimentary and Alternative Medicine, "CAM and Hepatitis C: A Focus on Herbal

Supplements," http://nccam.nih.gov/health/hepatitisc/hepatitiscfacts.htm (accessed January 24, 2011).
6. Ibid.
7. Ibid.

Chapter 10

1. T. C. Li et al., "Hepatitis E Transmission From Wild Boar Meat," *Emerging Infectious Diseases* 11, 12 (December 2005): 1958–1960.
2. National Institute of Allergy and Infectious Disease, "Hepatitis E Vaccine: A Time of Testing," August 30, 2007, http://www.niaid.nih.gov/topics/hepatitis/hepatitisE/Pages/nepalHepEVaccine.aspx (accessed January 24, 2011).

Glossary

Acute—Starting suddenly and not lasting long.

Acute viral hepatitis—Initial short-term stage of hepatitis.

Alanine aminotransferase—Enzyme involved in the normal chemical processing of the amino acid alanine, which converts it to carbon dioxide and water and provides useful energy for the cell.

ALT—See **Alanine aminotransferase.**

Antibodies—Proteins produced by the immune system in response to antigens to fight a foreign body.

Antigens—Proteins that signal the presence of a substance foreign to the immune system.

Apoptosis—A pattern of cell death affecting individual cells.

B cells—Cells of the immune system that are responsible for humoral (body fluid) immunity.

Bile—A yellow to green-brown fluid secreted by the liver that is necessary for the digestion of fats.

Bile duct, hepatic—A tube that conveys bile from the liver to the gallbladder.

Biliary atresia—A congenital narrowing of the ducts that carry bile to the gallbladder from the liver causing the bile to back up into the liver and damage it.

Bilirubin—Orange-yellow bile pigment, which is a product of the breakdown of red blood cells.

Bloodborne—Transmitted only through the blood.

Budding—Process in which a virus pushes outward on the host cell membrane and the membrane folds around the capsid.

Canaliculi—Very small vessels.

Capsid—Protective protein coat for a viral nucleic acid.

Capsomer—Protein subunits that make up a capsid.

Carrier—A person who is infected but shows no symptoms and, in the case of hepatitis, can spread the virus.

Chronic hepatitis—Long-standing hepatitis infection.

Cirrhosis—A form of advanced liver degeneration.

Clinical disease—An illness that causes symptoms that require treatment by a medical professional.

Clinical sign—An abnormality caused by a disease that can be discovered by a doctor's examination of a patient.

Coagulation—The process of blood clotting.

Coinfection—Infection by two different microbes at the same time.

Complement proteins—Proteins produced by the liver that help antibodies attack foreign substances.

Core antigen—An antigen in the viral capsid that is part of the "core" or essential structure of the virus.

Cytoplasm—Substance that makes up the interior of a cell.

DNA—Deoxyribonucleic acid; a nucleic acid molecule that carries coded genetic information.

Endemic—Common or always present in a specific geographical area.

Enteric—Within or pertaining to the intestine.

Envelope—A membrane that encloses the nucleocapsid of some viruses.

Epitope—Small structural part of an antigen, which determines when a foreign substance is present.

Fulminant hepatitis—Sudden, extremely severe liver inflammation.

Genotype—Genetic constitution of an individual organism.

Helper T cell—Type of immune cell. Helper T cells act as guardians of the body and activate killer T and B cells.

Hemolytic anemia—An abnormal decrease in red blood cells, caused by their destruction.

Hepatic artery—The artery that supplies the liver with blood.

Hepatic encephalopathy—Brain disorder caused by a shrinking, malfunctioning liver.

Hepatic vein—Any of the veins that carries blood brought by the hepatic artery and the portal veins away from the liver. Humans usually have three hepatic veins.

Hepatocellular carcinoma—Cancer of the liver cells.

Hepatocytes—Cells that take materials from the blood, modify them, and deliver them along with new materials back to the blood.

Hepatomegaly—Enlarged liver.

Humoral—Pertaining to body fluids.

Humoral response—An immune response that involves only antibodies in the body fluids.

Icosahedron—A polygon with 20 sides.

Icteric phase—Phase of hepatitis infection in which the skin and sclerae (the whites of the eyes) turn yellow.

Immunity—The state of being non-susceptible to a particular condition or disease.

Immunoglobulin—Any of five classes of structurally distinct antibodies in the serum.

Incidence—The number of new cases of a disease per year for a specified number of people.

Incubation phase—Span of time from the initial infection until the appearance of symptoms.

Inflammation—A protective response of tissues to injury. It is characterized by pain, redness, swelling, and heat.

Interferon—Specialized protein produced by some cells that "interferes" with viral replication.

Jaundice—A condition of high bilirubin with yellowing of the skin.

Killer T cells—Immune cells that are activated by helper T cells that identify, attack, and destroy infected cells.

Liver biopsy—The process of taking a living tissue sample from a patient's liver for examination with a microscope. Samples may be obtained by brushing the surface of the tissue, or cutting a piece of tissue off with a scalpel or scissors. A liver biopsy is done with special needle and requires minor surgery and local anesthesia. There is a small risk of damage to the lungs or gallbladder, as well as a risk of infection.

Lobes, hepatic—Portions of the liver.

Lobules—Small lobes.

Lysis—A sudden opening-up of a cell to release its contents, something like an explosion; lysis kills cells.

Macrophages—Large cells that originate in the bone marrow and are found throughout the body. They are scavengers of tissue debris and dead cells.

Major histocompatibility complex (MHC)—A special protein on the surface of cells that holds onto epitopes that can be recognized by killer T cells.

Microbe—Any very small organism such as a bacterium or virus that does not have a nucleus.

Nonreplicative phase—Period during which the virus stops reproducing itself and viremia has decreased to a minimal level.

Nucleic acid—Compound within a cell that is involved in determination and transmission of genetic characteristics. There are two kinds: DNA and RNA.

Nucleocapsid—Viral nucleic acid that is enclosed by a capsid.

Outbreak—Sudden increase of disease in a specific geographic area.

Pandemic—A wide epidemic that spreads over continents.

Parenteral transmission—Introduction of substances into the body by injection into the bloodstream.

Pegylated—Man-made type of interferon, used to treat hepatitis C infection.

Phagocytes—Cells specialized for engulfing and destroying other cells and foreign substances.

Phagocytosis—The mechanism by which phagocytes engulf substances.

Polyprotein—A protein composed of many different proteins linked together end to end.

Portal vein—Vein that supplies blood drained from the intestines to the liver.

Prevalence—Number of all cases of a disease, new and old, per year in a given population.

Prodromal phase—Period of onset of nonspecific disease symptoms.

Proliferation—Cell division, multiplication, and growth.

Proteins—Molecules made up of specific sequences of amino acids that are chemically linked. They are the functional and structural units of cells.

Recovery phase—The final disease phase of an acute infection in which the immune system ultimately overcomes the virus and symptoms fade away.

Regenerate—Rebuild and restore the original structure and function of a damaged tissue, starting with only a remnant of the original tissue, without any external help.

Replicative phase—Period during which the virus reproduces itself and infects healthy cells.

RNA—Ribonucleic acid; a nucleic acid molecule that is involved directly in protein synthesis.

Satellite virus—A virus with a capsid that requires the help of another virus to reproduce. Because it is less complete than the helper virus and is always found in its presence, it is referred to as a satellite.

Self-limited—When the body's immune system defeats a viral infection.

Seroconversion phase—Period during which the immune system attacks and destroys about 10% of infected liver cells each year; usually characterized by no symptoms and less viremia.

Serum—The thin liquid part of whole blood that remains after all blood cells and clotting materials are removed.

Sinus—A cavity, channel, or hollow.

Sinusoids—Small sinuses.

Superinfection—An infection by a new microbe that occurs after an earlier infection has occurred and is in a chronic phase.

Symptoms—Evidence of disease that is reported by the patient, such as a headache or fatigue.

T lymphocytes—White blood cells that are present at high levels in special organs called lymph nodes and are produced in the thymus gland.

Transcription—Process of copying or transcribing the codons in a gene to start synthesis of the protein encoded by that gene.

Viral nucleic acid—Nucleic acid molecule present in a virus that carries coded genetic information that allows for the reproduction of viruses similar to itself.

Viremia—Viruses in the blood.

Virion—The virus structure that exits a host cell and is able to infect other cells.

Further Resources

Books

Bader, T. F. *Viral Hepatitis. Practical Evaluation and Treatment,* 3rd ed. Cambridge, Mass.: Hogrefe and Huber, 2001.

Bruce, Cara, Lisa Montanarelli, and Teresa Wright. *The First Year: Hepatitis C: An Essential Guide for the Newly Diagnosed.* Cambridge, Mass.: Marlowe & Company, 2007.

Delirious, Johnny. *Hepatitis C, Cured.* Bloomington, Ind.: AuthorHouse, 2009.

Duncan, Tim, and Catherine Olivolo. *Conquering Hepatitis C and Surviving Treatment: An Essential Guide Through Every Step of the HCV Treatment Process.* HCVShare.org, 2010.

Everson, Gregory T., and Hedy Weinberg. *Living with Hepatitis B: A Survivor's Guide.* Long Island City, N.Y.: Hatherleigh Press, 2002.

———. *Living with Hepatitis C: A Survivor's Guide*, 3rd ed. Long Island City, N.Y.: Hatherleigh Press, 2002.

Gish, Robert, Ruth Misha, and Kalia Doner. *The Hepatitis C Health Book.* New York: St. Martin's Press, 2007.

Gray, Vickie. *The Silver Dragon: Hepatitis Awareness Poetry.* Booksurge.com, 2008.

Koff, Raymond S., and George Y. Wu. *Chronic Viral Hepatitis. Diagnosis and Therapeutics.* Totowa, N.J.: Humana Press, 2001.

Muhammad, Kevin. *The Case Against Hepatitis B Vaccination: Prevent Your Infants and Newborns from Being Permanently Injured.* Newark, Del.: Tech-Doc, 2009.

Napolitano, Ralph. *Hepatitis C Survival Secrets: With Critical Insights Your Doctor Won't Share.* Pine Bush, N.Y.: HTX Enterprises, 2010.

Palmer, Melissa. *Guide to Hepatitis & Liver Disease: What You Need to Know.* New York: Avery Publishing Group, 2004.

Parr, Elizabeth. *I'm Glad You're Not Dead: A Liver Transplant Story.* Gloucester, Mass.: Journey Publishing, 2000.

Radetsky, P. *The Invisible Invaders: Viruses and the Scientists Who Pursue Them.* Boston: Little, Brown and Company, 1991.

Regis, E. *Virus Ground Zero: Stalking the Killer Viruses with the Centers for Disease Control.* New York: Pocket Books, 1996.

Tibbs, Christopher J. *Clinicians' Guide to Viral Hepatitis*. London: Arnold Publishers, 2001.

Wagner, E. K., and M. J. Hewlett. *Basic Virology.* Ames, lowa: Blackwell Science, 1999.

Zimmerman, Barry E., and David J. Zimmerman. *Killer Germs*. New York: McGraw-Hill/Contemporary Books, 1996.

Web Sites

All the links to every possible question you may have about viruses, by Professor David Sander of Tulane University
http://www.tulane.edu/~dmsander/garryfavweb.html

Centers for Disease Control and Prevention, Viral Hepatitis
http://www.cdc.gov/hepatitis

emedicinehealth, Hepatitis A
http://www.emedicinehealth.com/hepatitis_a/article_em.htm

The Euroliver Foundation educational materials about liver diseases
http://www.hepatitis.org/accueilangl.htm

Florida Department of Health, Hepatitis Prevention Program
http://www.doh.state.fl.us/disease_ctrl/aids/hep/index.html

Hepatitis B Foundation
http://www.hepb.org/

Hepatitis C, Many links to sites devoted to hepatitis
http://www.hepatitis-c.de/linkse.htm

Hepatitis Foundation International
http://www.hepfi.org

The Liver Foundation educational materials
http://www.liverfoundation.org/db-home/articles

The Mayo Clinic, Hepatitis C
http://www.mayoclinic.com/health/hepatitis-c/DS00097/DSECTION%3Dtreatments-and-drugs

Medical News Today, What is Hepatitis?
http://www.medicalnewstoday.com/articles/145869.php

MedicineNet.com, Viral Hepatitis
http://www.medicinenet.com/viral_hepatitis/article.htm

Medline Plus, Hepatitis
http://www.nlm.nih.gov/medlineplus/ency/article/001154.htm
http://www.nlm.nih.gov/medlineplus/hepatitis.html

National Foundation for Infectious Diseases
http://www.nfid.org/pdf/factsheets/hepbadult.pdf

National Institute of Allergy and Infectious Diseases, Viral Hepatitis
http://www.niaid.nih.gov/topics/hepatitis/Pages/default.aspx

National Institutes of Health discussion of the immune system
http://www.niaid.nih.gov/final/immun/immun.htm

National Library of Medicine information
http://www.nlm.nih.gov/medlineplus/hepatitis.html

The *New York Times,* Hepatitis
http://health.nytimes.com/health/guides/disease/hepatitis/overview.html

U.S. Food and Drug Administration, Hepatitis A Virus
http://www.fda.gov/food/foodsafety/foodborneillness/foodborneillness foodbornepathogensnaturaltoxins/badbugbook/ucm071294.htm

Washington University School of Medicine, History of the discovery of virus structure by the Department of Molecular Microbiology
http://medschool.wustl.edu/~virology

WebMD, Hepatitis Health Center
http://www.webmd.com/hepatitis/default.htm

WomansHealth.gov, Viral Hepatitis
http://www.womenshealth.gov/faq/viral-hepatitis.cfm

World Health Organization, Hepatitis
http://www.who.int/csr/disease/hepatitis/en/index.html

Wrong Diagnosis, Fatigue as a symptom of hepatitis
http://www.wrongdiagnosis.com/sym/fatigue.htm

Index

About the Authors

Lyle W. Horn earned a Ph.D. from the Johns Hopkins University in 1970. He taught medical and dental students, graduate students, and undergraduate students in pharmacy, physical therapy, and nursing for 30 years. He has conducted research in his own laboratory, at the Woods Hole Marine Biological Laboratory, and at the National Institutes of Health. He has published original research articles in many scientific journals.

Dr. Horn is retired from teaching and research and is living with his wife, two greyhounds, a chow chow, and four cats in an early 19th-century farmhouse in central Pennsylvania, which he is busy restoring. He also does scientific consulting, medical writing and editing, and community service.

Dr. Alan Hecht is a practicing chiropractor in New York. He is also an adjunct professor at Farmingdale State College and Nassau Community College and an adjunct associate professor at the C.W. Post campus of Long Island University. He teaches courses in medical microbiology, health and human disease, anatomy and physiology, comparative anatomy, human physiology, embryology, and general biology. In addition he is the course coordinator for Human Biology at Hofstra University where he is an adjunct assistant professor.

Dr. Hecht received his B.S. in biology–pre medical studies from Fairleigh Dickinson University in Teaneck, New Jersy. He received his M.S. in basic medical sciences from New York University School of Medicine. He also received his Doctor of Chiropractic (D.C.) degree from New York Chiropractic College in Brookville, New York.

About the Consulting Editor

Hilary Babcock, M.D., M.P.H., is an assistant professor of medicine at Washington University School of Medicine and the Medical Director of Occupational Health for Barnes-Jewish Hospital and St. Louis Children's Hospital. She received her undergraduate degree from Brown University and her M.D. from the University of Texas Southwestern Medical Center at Dallas. After completing her residency, chief residency, and Infectious Disease fellowship at Barnes-Jewish Hospital, she joined the faculty of the Infectious Disease division. She completed an M.P.H. in Public Health from St. Louis University School of Public Health in 2006. She has lectured, taught, and written extensively about infectious diseases, their treatment, and their prevention. She is a member of numerous medical associations and is board certified in infectious disease. She lives in St. Louis, Missouri.